Chicken salad with boiled dressing
Benedictine salad
Sally Lunn
Secret strawberry shortcake
Bourbon ball torte

# Introduction

I suppose there are people in this world for whom the first Saturday in May is unimportant, who have never heard of the Triple Crown or the twin spires.

But in Louisville, and much of Kentucky, the first Saturday in May isn't a day, it is a week...no, two, and a little more if you back way up to the fireworks extravaganza Thunder Over Louisville. For people who live in Louisville, Kentucky Derby celebrations go on and on and on—with balls and balloon races, half-marathons and parades, bed races and boat races and a whole lot more.

As the actual first Saturday in May approaches, however, the festivities heat up. House guests often arrive, perhaps as a couple of friends, perhaps as carloads of your children's friends from college, perhaps as a business acquaintance who must be entertained. For that, there are outdoor "chuck wagons" with live music and vendors selling food, there is a hot-air balloon race the Saturday previous to the Derby, a golf tournament and so on.

On Wednesday evening, the Belle of Louisville and the Delta Queen—two stern-wheeled river boats—race in what we call The Great Steamboat race. On-lookers line what river banks they can, anyone with a house on the river has a party, high-rise office towers hold revelers on their river-view sides. In general, the food is casual— picnic and potluck.

On Thursday, spectators line Broadway for the Pegasus Parade, complete with floats, bands and at least one visiting celebrity as master of ceremonies.

Friday racing at Churchill Downs includes the running of the Kentucky Oaks, called "the Oaks," by natives, many of whom choose to attend the races that day, and stay out of the slightly crazier crowds on Derby day. For many years, the Oaks was attended by a largely hometown crowd, appreciative and fun-loving. The county schools are closed that day, and people take off work. If they aren't actually going to the races, they may be entertaining, or getting ready to entertain.

Oaks day is a big day for entertaining. The restaurants are packed and people have parties that night—fancy dinner parties, cocktail parties, casual get-togethers. As Christmas Eve is to Christmas, the Oaks is to the Derby.

How you celebrate Derby Day depends on your circumstances. If you are wealthy, a celebrity, have business interests in major international corporations, have a well-established Louisville family or business, or are simply lucky, you might have prime Derby tickets. Then you might host or attend a Derby brunch, so that you can eat early and leave for the track in time for the first race of the day. If you are young and/or adventurous or a dedicated Derby lover, you may end up in the infield, where the crowd is notoriously wilder, despite the recent security restrictions on the food and drink you can carry in. The infield is completely exposed to weather, the lines for the restrooms are long, and from many—perhaps most—spots you cannot see the horses as they race around the track. But it is the place to be for those who love a party atmosphere. Infielders try to eat a good breakfast, and take lunch in with them.

Others celebrate the Derby at home, with large or small parties. House parties can include caterers, bartenders and waiters, rented tables and chairs and tents. Or they might have a pot luck with friends and neighbors, limited to those who fit in your house.

My friends who had Derby pot lucks for many years added the line "children welcome unless it's raining" to their invitations. They provided one mint julep for everyone that would be passed around at about the time the horses were leaving the paddock area. Everyone chipped in regular pot luck foods—seven-layer dip and cheese balls—not so much attention was paid to traditional foods. Beer and sodas were the most common drinks; a few people brought wine.

Televisions were set up at different locations around the house. When the horses were led onto the track and the band played "My Old Kentucky Home," everyone sang, some cried. Everyone watched attentively as the horses were loaded into the starting gate and the race ensued. Two minutes later, the person who drew the correct name out of a basket was given his or her winnings, and the party started again.

For many years I lived out of town, first in Florida, then in Washington, D.C. During those years I would give Derby parties, sometimes with expatriate friends who needed

no explanations and fell quickly into the rituals, other times with non-Kentuckians who wondered what everything was and wrinkled their noses at the strong taste of my mint julep.

At all of these parties there is some obligatory gambling, from complicated parimutuel systems to picking names out of a hat – many hats, if there are many people, and many prices, if that appeals to the high rollers.

After Saturday, there may still be a need for socializing and comradery. If your house is full of overnight guests, they must be fed. If you've been too busy for friends during the festivities – and Derby time means a heavy work schedule for some people— Sunday is a good time to hold or attend a quiet, more intimate brunch.

Then it's over. Another Derby has run its course. Another winner named. Guests leave. Everyone's worn out, but next year it will all happen again.

# Derby Entertaining

Derby food is a little like Thanksgiving food—there are traditions that must be honored but there's always room for new and creative ideas. The season affects Derby menus, too—asparagus, lettuce and spinach, mint, and strawberries are either in season or on the cusp, and therefore always appear on Derby buffet tables. Some foods become traditional because they're practical and universally loved.

With guests feeling curious and adventurous, they are more open to tasting grits and country ham. Because all eyes are focused on Kentucky traditions, people are interested in the stories behind Derby Pie, Henry Bain Sauce and Benedictine. The menus we've set out here honor virtually all those Derby traditions, and relate some of the stories that go with them. Feel free to mix and match the recipes to fit your party plan and your own tastes.

If you are hosting house guests, you need to be well-organized and have lots of food available. Don't worry that every morsel have a Derby theme attached to it. When you're planning three days of menus you can rely on your standard dishes, say, spaghetti and meat loaf, while tossing in a few items with Kentucky flavor; serve Henry Bain Sauce with the meat loaf, or a Derby Pie for dessert.

Cooking for large groups of people requires more than just large recipes. It also requires lots of pans and dishes, especially if you're cooking ahead and freezing food. For instance, the 9-by 13-inch casserole is a common household pan and we call for it a lot. Check to see that you have enough to hold what you're preparing. In addition, you may think that the common 9-by 13-inch pan may not be attractive enough to serve as an oven-to-table container, so you may want to plan ahead for using something more decorative. Read the recipes through, think about the dishes you'll need for cooking and serving, then borrow or rent anything you might not have.

In Louisville, the crowd descending on your home for several years of Derby entertaining may be a bunch of college kids. If that's the case at your house, you're on your own as far as serving sizes go. Fill a house with 19-year-old boys and there is no such thing as too much food.

Cooking ahead makes entertaining a lot easier. Many of the recipes we've included in this book can be made and frozen, or prepared several weeks or days before your meal. Others, while they can't be made and frozen, can be made in stages to make final preparation either quick for you or easy for your child or houseguest.

For more information about the Kentucky Derby or Kentucky Derby-related events, get in touch with people who are in the Kentucky Derby business, such as:

• The Kentucky Derby Museum. This museum is on the grounds of Churchill Downs and is one of the state's most popular tourist destinations. Through it you can order all the essentials for your Derby parties, including Derby-themed invitations, tableware and decorations, in addition to books and other cookbooks. Reach it at www.derbymuseum.org.

• The Kentucky Derby Festival is the official entity under whose auspices Derby events happen. From Thunder over Louisville to the Mini Marathon, histories and details are provided at www.kdf.org.

# A Boat Race Picnic

The Great Steamboat Race, generally between the Belle of Louisville and the Delta Queen, is one of the oldest Derby traditions and is always held on the Wednesday before Derby.

It is just one of many opportunities for picnicking during the Kentucky Derby Festival. About two weeks before the actual horse race, Louisville officially begins its Kentucky Derby Festival with Thunder Over Louisville, a grandiose fireworks display that occurs over the Ohio River and requires an all-day commitment to get your favorite seat on the waterfront. People find their spots in the morning and don't move. Those people are serious picnickers.

But the boat race is a time for relaxed and casual entertaining on both sides of the river. At Louisville's old waterworks, now owned by the Louisville Visual Arts Association, people pay handsomely for seats and sometimes pack elegant dinners. Down the road at Cox Park, picnickers lay their blankets on the ground.

Tuna sandwiches and chips will suffice adequately—not to mention KFC buckets, which you see plenty of—but here we're offering a few of our favorite portable foods for a sustaining repast.

## BOAT RACE PICNIC

THERMOS OF PEA SOUP
SESAME-CHICKPEA DINNER WRAPS
CALIFORNIA CHICKEN WRAPS
BEEF CAESAR WRAPS
QUICK SALSA FOR CHIPS
TOFFEE-NUT OATMEAL COOKIES
SESAME BARS

---

**THERMOS PEA SOUP**

If the weather is warm, serve the soup cold. If it's cold out (it has snowed on more than one Derby Day), heat the soup.

2 TABLESPOONS VEGETABLE OIL
1 MEDIUM ONION, CHOPPED
1 TABLESPOON CURRY POWDER
1/2 TEASPOON TABASCO
1/2 TEASPOON SALT
1/4 TEASPOON (FRESHLY GROUND) BLACK PEPPER
3 10-OUNCE PACKAGES FROZEN PEAS (SUBSTITUTE 2 POUNDS FRESH SHELLED PEAS)
4 CUPS CHICKEN BROTH, WATER OR COMBINATION
1/2 CUP SOUR CREAM

Heat vegetable oil in a saucepan set over medium-high heat. Add chopped onions and, stirring occasionally, cook about 5 minutes or until onions are soft and translucent. Add curry powder, Tabasco, salt, and pepper and stir to coat onions. Add peas and chicken broth and bring to a boil. Remove from heat and blend in batches in a blender until smooth. Strain if desired. Taste and add more salt if necessary. Stir in sour cream or low-fat sour cream. Pour into Thermos (if serving soup hot, pre-heat Thermos with boiling water before filling). Makes about 8 cups.

## SESAME-CHICKPEA DINNER WRAPS

1/4 CUP SESAME SEEDS

3 TABLESPOONS OLIVE OIL

JUICE OF 1 LEMON

1 TABLESPOON FRESH BASIL OR 1 TEASPOON DRY BASIL

1 TEASPOON SALT

1 TEASPOON MINCED GARLIC, ABOUT 2 CLOVES

1/2 TEASPOON (FRESHLY GROUND) BLACK PEPPER

4 CUPS SLIVERED ROMAINE LETTUCE

1 RED BELL PEPPER, FINELY CHOPPED

15 TO 19 OUNCES CANNED CHICKPEAS

8 OUNCES FETA CHEESE

8 10-INCH FLOUR TORTILLAS

Toast sesame seeds in a 350-degree oven (for about 15 minutes) or in a dry skillet on top of the stove (stir frequently) until they are golden and aromatic.

Meanwhile, mix olive oil, lemon juice, basil, salt, garlic, and pepper in a small bowl. Combine romaine and red bell pepper in a large bowl. Drain canned chickpeas and coarsely chop them. Crumble feta cheese. Add cheese and beans to the salad bowl. Sprinkle with sesame seeds. Drizzle with lemon juice mixture and toss to blend evenly. If you have an electric stove, set a dry non-stick skillet over medium high heat and cook tortillas on each side for about 15 seconds (a total of 30 seconds). If you have a gas stove, put the tortilla right on the flame and flip it constantly until it is warm and slightly pliable. Stack the tortillas as you finish them.

Dip about 1 cup of lettuce mixture onto the warm tortillas to form a 2- by 5-inch rectangle toward the bottom center. Fold up the bottom edge of the tortilla to nearly cover the filling. Fold in both sides, then finish rolling the tortilla to enclose filling.

Makes 8 large wraps that aren't too filling—probably 2 per person. You can make these wraps hours ahead. Wrap individually in plastic wrap and refrigerate. Leftovers keep well for a couple of days.

## CALIFORNIA CHICKEN WRAPS

1/3 CUP GOOD QUALITY REAL MAYONNAISE

JUICE OF 1 LIME

1 OR 2 GARLIC CLOVES, PEELED AND MINCED, 1/2 TO 1 TEASPOON

SALT AND (FRESHLY GROUND) BLACK PEPPER TO TASTE

1 1/2 POUNDS BONED AND SKINNED CHICKEN BREAST HALVES

4 CUPS FINELY CHOPPED ROMAINE LETTUCE

1 TOMATO, SEEDED AND FINELY CHOPPED, ABOUT 1 CUP

1 RIPE AVOCADO IN 1/2-INCH DICE

8 10-INCH FLOUR TORTILLAS

Combine mayonnaise with lime juice, minced garlic and a little salt and pepper. Heat broiler and move rack to top shelf, or about 4 inches from heat.

Put 2 teaspoons of mayonnaise on the chicken breasts and smear it over them to coat them lightly. Place the chicken on a shallow baking sheet (or on broiler pan). Broil the chicken about 5 minutes on each side, or until just about done in the middle. Remove the pan from the oven and set aside.

Chop the lettuce. Combine with chopped tomato and avocado. Cut the chicken in 1/2-inch dice and mix it with the lettuce.

Warm the tortillas directly over a gas flame or in a dry skillet on an electric burner. Warming each should take about 15 to 30 seconds. Turn the tortilla over and over again until it is just warm and pliable. Stack and repeat until finished.

Smear a little mayonnaise on each tortilla before adding filling. Divide the filling among the tortillas, placing about 1 cup of filling in a wide strip a little below the center. Fold up the bottom edge of the tortilla to nearly cover the filling. Fold in both sides, then finish rolling the tortilla to enclose filling.

You can make these wraps hours ahead. Wrap individually in plastic wrap and refrigerate. Leftovers keep well for a couple of days.

Makes 8 medium-sized wraps.

## BEEF CAESAR WRAPS

> 1/4 CUP PARMESAN CHEESE, PREFERABLY FRESHLY GRATED
> 1/3 CUP GOOD QUALITY REAL MAYONNAISE
> JUICE OF 1/2 LEMON
> 1 OR 2 GARLIC CLOVES, PEELED AND MINCED, 1/2 TO 1 TEASPOON
> 1 TEASPOON WORCESTERSHIRE SAUCE
> SALT AND (FRESHLY GROUND) BLACK PEPPER TO TASTE
> 1 TO 1 1/2 POUNDS FLANK STEAK
> 6 CUPS FINELY CHOPPED ROMAINE LETTUCE
> 1 TOMATO, SEEDED AND FINELY CHOPPED, ABOUT 1 CUP
> 8 10-INCH FLOUR TORTILLAS

Combine cheese, mayonnaise, lemon juice, garlic, Worcestershire and salt and pepper. Heat broiler and move rack to top shelf, or about 4 inches from heat. Lightly season the meat with salt and pepper, then spread with about 2 teaspoons of dressing.

Place flank steak on a shallow baking sheet. Score about 1/16-inch deep in a diamond pattern on both sides. Broil about 7 minutes on each side, or to desired doneness (flank steak is best rare or medium rare). Remove the pan from the oven and set aside.

Finely chop the lettuce and the tomato. Slice the steak very thinly on the diagonal to make long thin strips. Mix it with the remaining dressing.

Warm the tortillas directly over a gas flame or in a dry skillet on an electric burner. Warming each should take about 15 to 30 seconds. Turn the tortilla over and over again until it is just warm and pliable. Stack and repeat until finished.

Divide the filling among the tortillas, placing a few strips of steak on 1 tortilla, covering with a generous 1/2 cup of lettuce and a sprinkling of tomatoes. Fold up the bottom edge of the tortilla to nearly cover the filling. Fold in both sides, then finish rolling the tortilla to enclose filling.

You can make these wraps hours ahead, wrapping them tightly in plastic wrap.

Makes 8 medium-sized wraps.

## QUICK SALSA

> 1 JAR PREPARED SALSA (ABOUT 16 OUNCES)
> 1 CLOVE GARLIC, MINCED, ABOUT 1/2 TEASPOON
> JUICE OF 1 LIME
> 1/4 CUP MINCED, FRESH CILANTRO (APPROXIMATELY)

Combine ingredients. Makes about 2 cups. Serve with tortilla chips or with Mexican or Tex Mex main courses, including the egg casserole on page 35.

## TOFFEE-NUT OATMEAL COOKIES

> 1 CUP BUTTER, SLIGHTLY SOFTENED
> 1 CUP BROWN SUGAR
> 1/2 CUP SUGAR
> 2 EGGS
> 1 1/2 CUPS ALL-PURPOSE FLOUR
> 1 TEASPOON BAKING SODA
> 1/2 TEASPOON SALT
> 3 CUPS ROLLED OATS (QUICK OR OLD-FASHIONED)
> 1 CUP TOFFEE BRICKLE CHIPS
> 1 CUP CHOPPED PECANS, OPTIONAL

Heat oven to 350 degrees. Beat butter until creamy. Add sugars and beat again until blended. Add eggs and beat well. Add flour, soda and salt and beat until mixed well. Stir in oats, brickle chips and pecans, if using. Drop by rounded tablespoons on an ungreased cookie sheet and bake 12 to 15 minutes until golden brown. Makes about 2 dozen.

## Sesame bars

> 1/2 CUP UNSALTED BUTTER
> 1 CUP BROWN SUGAR
> 1 EGG
> 1 TEASPOON VANILLA
> 1 CUP ALL-PURPOSE FLOUR
> 1/4 TEASPOON BAKING POWDER
> 1/8 TEASPOON SALT
> 1 1/2 CUPS TOASTED SESAME SEEDS (SEE NOTE)

Beat butter until soft and fluffy. Add sugar, beating constantly, until well-blended. Add egg and vanilla and beat to combine.

Add flour, baking powder and salt. Use a wooden spoon to blend this in to the butter mixture. Stir in sesame seeds. Press into an 8-inch square pan and bake 45 minutes at 350 degrees. Cut into small bars. Makes 20 to 24.

NOTE: To toast sesame seeds, spread them in a large, flat pan with shallow sides and put in a 350-degree oven for 15 minutes, or until the seeds are light brown. Stir several times, being careful about moving them out of corners, which tend to hold heat. Cool completely before stirring into cookie batter.

# FEEDING A HOUSE PARTY

The most serious Derby partying, perhaps, is when your nearly-adult children arrive home from college with friends in tow, delirious about showing them what Louisville is like in spring and what the most famous two minutes in sports is all about. This is when you remember that young adults are big, and their metabolisms are on overdrive.

That's when it's good to have a plan to have food cooked ahead, food that can stay in the refrigerator and be dished out when the urge hits, hunks of meat that can be carved for sandwiches, giant pots of soup that can be reheated bowl by bowl in the microwave.

# DERBY 101

A Guide to Food and Menus
For Kentucky Derby Week

# Contents

*To John, Eliza and Martin. All my love.*

# DERBY 101

## A Guide to Food and Menus
## For Kentucky Derby Week

### SARAH FRITSCHNER

For this situation, we've provided a guide for what you might serve. For Thursday night, when the crowd rolls in, we offer a roast pork and several sturdy salads that can stand up to staggered feedings. You might substitute roast turkey breast, or beef, provide supermarket potato salad and slaw, a bakery cake or cookies.

And so it goes. Planning is the most difficult part of a multi-day slumber party where people move in great waves of comings and goings. Be flexible, be prepared, and be ready to let them do some of the work.

Before you make anything for lunch to be carried into the Downs, call and ask about restrictions on what may and may not be brought through the gates, and how it

## THURSDAY NIGHT

Pork loin with herb rub and horseradish sauce
Blue cheese coleslaw
Pepper slaw vinaigrette
German potato salad for a crowd
Potato refrigerator rolls
Cissy Gregg's buttermilk pound cake with chocolate or caramel sauce

## FRIDAY BREAKFAST

Savory egg and sausage casserole
Fried apples
Scones

## FRIDAY TRACK SNACKS

Pork roast sandwiches
Beer cheese and crackers
Raw veggies with Mediterranean dip
Derby brownies

## FRIDAY EVENING

Karen's sloppy Joes
Portobelo sandwiches with red onion jam
Orzo salad
Sugar snap pea salad
Peanut butter chocolate chip oatmeal cookies
Chicken tetrazzini
Pan-fried herbed cherry tomatoes
Strawberry feta spinach salad
Corn muffins
Best caramel cake

## SATURDAY BREAKFAST

Bacon for a crowd
French toast for a crowd
Strawberry sauce for French toast (and for leftover pound cake)

## SATURDAY AT THE TRACK
Derby club sandwiches
Tuna salad
Chocolate cherry bars

## SATURDAY DINNER
Pepper sausage and chicken
Cheesy ziti
Garlic bread
Tossed salad with best mustard vinaigrette
Mary's chocolate pie

## SUNDAY BRUNCH
Hot brown casserole
Bourbon buttermilk pie with strawberries

## THURSDAY NIGHT

PORK LOIN WITH HERB RUB

This pork loin recipe is my ace-in-the-hole for any large gathering—whether it be Derby weekend, a summer neighbor party or Thanksgiving when a passel of relatives comes to stay. Leftovers make great sandwiches, and we depend on them here for Friday lunch at the track. If you need more pork, just double the recipe. You won't need to increase cooking time unless your roasts are closely situated in the oven—if they're packed together, it takes longer for the heat to penetrate. And remember, a meat thermometer is always the safest bet for knowing when roasted meat is perfectly cooked.

If you don't have an electric coffee grinder for grinding spices, consider getting one; they are immensely useful if you like to cook, especially for summer grilling. Otherwise, a blender will do. If you'd like an easier route, substitute ground cumin for the fennel seeds. Ground coriander is easy to find in supermarket spice racks. Combine these with ground black pepper and you won't need to grind anything.

2 TEASPOONS DRIED BASIL
2 TEASPOONS DRIED THYME
2 TEASPOONS DRIED OREGANO
1 TABLESPOON FENNEL SEEDS
1 TEASPOON CORIANDER (PREFERABLY WHOLE)
1 TABLESPOON SALT, PREFERABLY KOSHER SALT
2 TEASPOONS WHOLE BLACK PEPPERCORNS
1 TABLESPOON FRESH MINCED GARLIC (OR PRE-MINCED GARLIC FROM A JAR)
1 7-POUND PORK LOIN CUT INTO 2 PIECES TO MAKE 2 SHORTER ROASTS

Combine basil, thyme, oregano, fennel, coriander, salt and peppercorns in a spice grinder or blender and grind to a coarse powder.Rub the minced garlic all over the pork roasts. Sprinkle each with spice mix and rub all over to coat. To cook the pork in the oven: Put the roasts on a rack set in a shallow roasting pan. Place pan in 325-degree oven until a meat thermometer registers 155 degrees, about 60 minutes. To cook on the grill: Prepare a charcoal grill by stacking coals on one side (or heat one side of a gas grill). When the coals are hot, put the pork roast on the side without the coals, cover the grill and cook the roasts about 60 minutes, or until a thermometer registers 155 degrees. Let the roasts sit 10 minutes before you carve them into thin slices.Serve with horseradish sauce. Serves 16. (Leftovers make great sandwiches.)

## HORSERADISH SAUCE

    1 CUP (8 OUNCES) SOUR CREAM
    2 TABLESPOONS EUROPEAN-STYLE MUSTARD
    2 TABLESPOONS BOTTLED HORSERADISH
    1 CLOVE GARLIC, MINCED, ABOUT 1/2 TEASPOON

Combine sauce ingredients and stir to mix thoroughly. Makes about 1 1/4 cups.

## BLUE CHEESE COLESLAW

DRESSING:
    3 TABLESPOONS CIDER VINEGAR
    3 TABLESPOONS SUGAR
    1/2 CUP MAYONNAISE
    1/3 CUP SOUR CREAM
    2 TEASPOONS SALT
    1/2 TEASPOON (FRESHLY GROUND) BLACK PEPPER
    2 TEASPOONS DIJON MUSTARD
    2 TEASPOONS WORCESTERSHIRE SAUCE
    1/2 TEASPOON TABASCO, OR TO TASTE
    4 OUNCES BLUE CHEESE

SLAW:
    1 MEDIUM HEAD CABBAGE, ABOUT 1 1/2 POUNDS
    1 CUP CHOPPED RED CABBAGE
    1 CARROT, PEELED AND GRATED
    1/2 CUP FINELY CHOPPED FRESH PARSLEY
    1 BUNCH GREEN ONIONS, TRIMMED AND MINCED

To make the dressing: Put vinegar and sugar in a medium bowl. Add remaining ingredients, except cheese. Beat well to mix thoroughly and dissolve sugar and salt. Crumble cheese into the dressing and stir to mix. Set aside as you make the slaw, or refrigerate.

To make the slaw: Cut cabbage in half, then in quarters. Make a diagonal slice to remove the core from each section. Slice the cabbage as thinly as you can, placing sliced cabbage in a large bowl as you slice. Add remaining ingredients to the cabbage in the bowl. Gently toss to mix evenly. Pour dressing over the slaw and stir to distribute. Serves 12.

## Pepper slaw vinaigrette

### Slaw:

> 1 medium head cabbage, about 1 1/2 pounds
> 3 red bell peppers
> 2 green peppers
> 3 carrots
> 1/2 cup thinly sliced red onion

### Vinaigrette:

> 3/4 cup olive oil
> 1/4 cup vinegar, any will do (apple cider is good)
> 1 1/2 teaspoons salt, or to taste
> 1 teaspoon dry mustard
> 1/2 teaspoon Tabasco, or to taste

To make the slaw: Cut cabbage in half, then in quarters. Make a diagonal slice to remove the core from each section. Slice the cabbage as thinly as you can, placing the cabbage in a large bowl as you slice. Remove core and seeds from peppers and slice the peppers as thinly as you can, adding them to the bowl as you do. Trim and grate the carrots and add them to the bowl along with slivered red onion. Mix together and refrigerate.

Mix the vinaigrette dressing in a bowl or jar and stir or shake to dissolve salt and distribute mustard. Pour over cabbage and stir to combine. Serves 12 or more.

## GERMAN POTATO SALAD

5 POUNDS WAXY POTATOES, SUCH AS RED-SKINNED OR ROUND WHITE
1 SMALL ONION
1 POUND BACON
1 CUP VINEGAR, ANY WILL DO
1 TABLESPOON SALT
3 TABLESPOONS SUGAR
1 TEASPOON BLACK PEPPER, PREFERABLY FRESHLY GROUND
1/2 CUP WATER

Bring a large pot (or 2 large pots) of water to a boil. Add washed potatoes, return the water to a boil, then reduce heat to simmer the potatoes until they are tender when pierced with the thin blade of a paring knife. Time varies with the size of the potatoes but they're usually cooked in 20 to 40 minutes. Drain potatoes and cool them until they are warm. Peel if desired (I generally don't). Peel and thinly slice the onion.

Thinly slice the potatoes and drop them in a bowl as you do. Every so often, sprinkle some of the onions over the potatoes, so you get a sort of layering effect. Potatoes can be covered and chilled at this point, for a day or two, but bring them back to room temperature before pouring warm dressing on them.

Dice bacon by cutting crosswise into thin strips. Place the bacon in a deep skillet or wide saucepan over medium heat and cook, stirring, until crisp. Remove the bacon to an absorbent surface. There should be about 1 cup bacon fat in the pan. If there isn't, add a little vegetable or olive oil. Add vinegar to the pan and stir to remove brown bits from the bottom. When the vinegar boils, add remaining ingredients, stirring to dissolve salt and sugar. Pour over warm or room temperature potatoes and stir to distribute evenly. Sprinkle with bacon bits. Serves 15.

POTATO REFRIGERATOR ROLLS

These rolls are incredibly tender and delicious, made so with the addition of mashed potatoes, eggs, and butter. Why go to the trouble? These rolls will make you a star. If you'd rather not, buy Sister Schubert's rolls from the freezer section of your supermarket.

In reality, you can delay the rising of any yeast dough by refrigerating it to slow down the action of the yeast. But this is the time honored Southern mixture, which generally yields a very, very soft dough. I've added a little extra flour to make the dough easier to handle.

2 MEDIUM-SIZED POTATOES, OR EQUIVALENT DEHYDRATED POTATOES, COOKED ACCORD-
    ING TO PACKAGED DIRECTIONS
1 PACKAGE DRY YEAST
1 CUP MILK
1 CUP BUTTER
1/2 CUP SUGAR
2 TEASPOONS SALT
3 EGGS
6 CUPS FLOUR (2 CUPS WHOLE WHEAT, IF DESIRED)

Peel and boil the potatoes until tender. Mash them well and set them aside to cool.

In a small bowl, dissolve the yeast in 1/4 cup lukewarm water and set aside. Pour milk into a small saucepan or bowl and bring to a boil on the stove or in the microwave. Pour into a large bowl and add 1/2 cup butter, cut into pieces. When it melts, add potatoes and blend until smooth. Stir in sugar and salt. When the mixture is lukewarm, beat the eggs and add stir them into the milk mixture; add yeast. Stir in 5 cups of flour and mix thoroughly. Work in another cup of flour and knead dough for 5 to 10 minutes. Cover the bowl with plastic wrap and refrigerate 8 hours (or overnight).

When ready to use, melt 1/4 cup butter in each of two 9- by 13-inch baking pans. Pull off a portion of the dough and drop it onto a well-floured surface. The dough will be somewhat sticky, so keep your hands covered with flour to roll the piece in a smooth ball about the size of a golf ball. Put the ball in the baking pan and turn it to get a little butter on top. Fill both pans with similar sized rolls. Cover with plastic wrap and let them rise 20 minutes. (You may delay baking by putting the rolls in the refrigerator at this point—they will rise, but more slowly, and will be ready to bake in a few hours).

Heat oven to 400 degrees. Bake rolls for 20 minutes, or until deep golden brown. When they come out of the oven brush with more butter to keep their tops super-tender. Makes about 4 dozen rolls.

### CISSY GREGG'S BUTTERMILK POUND CAKE

Cissy Gregg was the long-admired food editor of *The Courier-Journal*. She worked at the Louisville newspaper for 21 years, and was at the helm when its color food photos were included in the Sunday Magazine. Cissy was known for a chatty writing style and foolproof recipes that she tested and evaluated in the newspaper test kitchen.

Her buttermilk pound cake is my standby foolproof dessert. She described it as "a joy to make and a pleasure to behold." I never make it in a bundt pan, because I can't ever get it out. I use a plain tube pan—like one used for angel food cakes. Use whatever pan you feel confident using.

3 CUPS FLOUR
1/2 TEASPOON BAKING SODA
1/2 TEASPOON BAKING POWDER
3/4 TEASPOON SALT
1 CUP BUTTER, SOFTENED
2 CUPS SUGAR
4 EGGS
1 CUP BUTTERMILK

Heat oven to 350 degrees. Grease and flour a 9-inch tube pan or similar-size pan. Combine flour, soda, baking powder and salt and set aside.

Beat butter until creamy. Add sugar and beat thoroughly. Add eggs, one at a time, beating each one into the batter completely before adding the next.

Use a spatula or a spoon to stir in flour alternately with the buttermilk (3 additions of flour, 2 of buttermilk). Spoon into baking pan and bake for 70 minutes, or until cake tests done. Serve with ice cream and chocolate or caramel sauce. Or serve with fresh fruit and whipped cream, or pretty much however you like. It goes with anything. Serves 10 to 12.

## CARAMEL SAUCE

1/2 CUP SUGAR
2 TABLESPOONS WATER
1 CUP HEAVY (WHIPPING) CREAM
1 TEASPOON VANILLA, RUM OR BOURBON

Combine sugar and water in a deep, small saucepan. Cook over medium heat, stirring to dissolve sugar. Put a top on the pot and cook for 2 minutes, then remove the top and increase heat to medium-high. Allow the mixture to boil until it begins to darken. If it seems to darken unevenly, swirl the liquid to mix it a little, and continue to cook until the mixture is a nutty brown. Remove from heat, add cream (the mixture will splutter and spit) and return to the heat, stirring, until the caramel is dissolved, the mixture darkens and is the consistency of half-and-half. Reduce heat to low, if necessary, to reduce spillovers.

Cool for 3 to 5 minutes, remove from heat, then stir in the vanilla. Chill; the mixture will thicken considerably. Sauce may be served warm or cold. Reheat over low heat, in the microwave, or by putting the jar of sauce in a pan of hot water. Makes 1 1/2 cups. Serve with pound cake or ice cream, with apple pie or cobbler. Keeps pretty much forever in the fridge.

## EASY CHOCOLATE SAUCE

The French call this mixture a *ganache* (gah-NOSH) and make it thicker or thinner depending on whether they are using it to fill truffles, glaze cakes or use it as sauce. Add a tablespoon or two of bourbon to add a Kentucky flair.

1 CUP HEAVY (WHIPPING) CREAM
6 OUNCES SEMI-SWEET CHOCOLATE BITS

In the microwave or in a small saucepan, bring the cream to a boil. Remove from heat and add chocolate. Allow it to stand a minute, then stir chocolate to melt it and blend it into the cream. If chocolate does not melt completely, heat it very gently and stir again. Use immediately or chill (it thickens after chilling). Keeps well for a week refrigerated, then it starts to turn grainy.

## FRIDAY BREAKFAST

### SAVORY EGG AND SAUSAGE CASSEROLE

More a crustless quiche than a casserole, this is easy to make, especially if you buy your mushrooms pre-sliced and the garlic pre-minced. To get some of the chores out of the way, you can cook the sausage, mushrooms and garlic ahead and refrigerate or freeze until you need it for the casserole.

8 OUNCES HOT ITALIAN SAUSAGE (ABOUT 2 LINKS, OR IN BULK)
8 OUNCES SLICED MUSHROOMS
2 CLOVES GARLIC, MINCED OR ABOUT 1 TEASPOON
12 EGGS
1/2 CUP MILK
1/2 CUP TOMATO SALSA (FROM A JAR, OR QUICK SALSA ON PAGE 22)
1 POUND GRATED EXTRA SHARP CHEDDAR OR MONTEREY JACK CHEESE
1/2 TEASPOON SALT
1/2 TEASPOON FRESHLY GROUND PEPPER

Heat oven to 350 degrees. Spray or lightly oil a 9- by 13-inch baking pan.

Crumble the sausage into a large skillet and cook over medium heat until cooked through, breaking it up as it cooks. Add mushrooms and garlic and cook until mushrooms are browned, about 10 minutes. Scrape into baking pan.

Crack the eggs into a large bowl and beat well. Add milk, salsa, half the cheese, salt and pepper. Beat well. Pour over sausage. Sprinkle with remaining cheese. Bake the casserole about 40 minutes, or until just set.

Serves 10. Serve for breakfast with fried apples and scones.

## FRIED APPLES

There's no need to buy premium-priced, large apples for this recipe. Smaller apples in bags will work fine. Choose from Jonathan, Granny Smith, Golden Delicious and other firm, tart apples. A mixture is great if you have several types. Without the salt, the apples will taste a little flat.

1/2 CUP BUTTER OR MARGARINE

1 CUP BROWN SUGAR

1/2 TEASPOON CINNAMON

1/4 TEASPOON SALT

8 MEDIUM APPLES

1 TEASPOON VANILLA, OPTIONAL

JUICE OF 1 LEMON, OPTIONAL

Divide butter, sugar, cinnamon and salt between 2 wide skillets over low heat so the butter can melt while you prepare the apples. (An electric skillet should hold all the apples, so if you have one, use it for this.)

Peel the apples if you want (I don't) and cut them in quarters. Cut out their cores, then cut each quarter in 2 or 3 pieces lengthwise. Dice into small pieces and add them to the skillets as you do.

Increase the heat to medium-high. Stir the apples to coat them in melted butter. Cover them with lids and cook 5 minutes to soften them. Remove top and increase heat to medium high or high. Let syrup boil 5 or 10 minutes until apples are soft and the liquid is syrupy. Remove from heat and add vanilla and lemon juice, if desired.

Serves 10 to 12.

## SCONES

Scones are like biscuits, just a little richer and in a little different shape. Sprinkle them with cinnamon sugar before baking, if desired, or add bits of dried fruit to the dough to add more interest.

4 CUPS ALL-PURPOSE FLOUR

4 TEASPOONS BAKING POWDER

1/2 CUP SUGAR

1 TEASPOON SALT

1 CUP COLD BUTTER

2 EGGS

1 CUP HALF-AND-HALF

1/4 CUP MELTED BUTTER

Heat oven to 400 degrees. Lightly spray or oil two small or one large cookie sheet. In a large bowl, combine flour, baking powder, sugar, and salt. Stir briefly to mix. Cut cold butter into 16 small pieces and add to bowl. Use a pastry blender or 2 knives to cut the butter into the flour until the mixture resembles coarse meal. (This process can also be done in the food processor).

In a medium bowl, beat eggs, then add half-and-half and beat again. Pour into flour mixture and stir until ingredients are moistened and hold together. Divide the mixture in half and place one half on a floured surface. Knead 10 times or so, to smooth out the texture—it should resemble biscuit dough. Place the kneaded dough on cookie sheet and pat into an 8-inch round. Repeat the process with remaining dough. Cut each round across the diameter 4 times to create 8 pie-shaped pieces and pull them away from each other slightly.

Bake for 12 to 15 minutes, until the scones are golden brown. Remove from oven and brush with butter to keep their tops tender. Serves 16. Recipe may be halved easily.

## FRIDAY TRACK SNACKS

BEER CHEESE

Kentucky cookbook author Marion Flexner wrote this in her 1949 book, *Out of Kentucky Kitchens*:

"In the days when free lunches were served in Kentucky saloons with every 5-cent glass of beer, we were told of a wonderful Beer Cheese that decked every bar... It will keep for weeks in a covered jar in the icebox and is a boon to the busy house-keeper." Needless to say, it can be made way in advance of your party.

1 POUND EXTRA-SHARP CHEDDAR, GRATED

4 OUNCES BLUE CHEESE

1/2 CUP CREAM CHEESE

12 OUNCES BEER (THE AVERAGE BOTTLE OR CAN)

2 TABLESPOONS WORCESTERSHIRE SAUCE, OR MORE TO TASTE

2 CLOVES GARLIC, MINCED, ABOUT 1 TEASPOON

1 TEASPOON DRY MUSTARD

1/2 TEASPOON SALT, OR TO TASTE

1 TEASPOON TABASCO OR 1/2 TEASPOON CAYENNE OR TO TASTE

Combine ingredients and whiz in food processor or use a large, heavy mixer. The blender is slow going, but can be done in small batches. The spread should be smooth and should spread easily—not too thick. Add cream, milk or more beer if you like. Add extra liquid to make it more dippy and less spready. Makes about 4 cups.

MEDITERRANEAN DIP FOR VEGETABLES

1 JAR (10 OR 12 OUNCES) ROASTED AND PEELED RED BELL PEPPERS

2 TABLESPOONS BOTTLED PESTO

8 OUNCES CRUMBLED FETA CHEESE

8 OUNCES CREAM CHEESE

Put drained peppers into blender with pesto. Blend 10 seconds on high or until smooth. Add feta cheese; blend briefly. Cut cream cheese into 8 chunks and add them 1 at a time to blender, blending after each addition (scrape the sides each time). Serve as a dip for vegetables or crackers. Makes 3 cups.

## DERBY BROWNIES

Gilding the lily, we add nuts and semi-sweet morsels to a basic brownie recipe. Add a tablespoon of bourbon in addition to the vanilla if you like the taste.

4 OUNCES UNSWEETENED CHOCOLATE

1/2 CUP BUTTER

4 EGGS

2 CUPS SUGAR

1 TEASPOON VANILLA

1 CUP FLOUR

1/2 TEASPOON SALT

1 CUP CHOPPED PECANS

1 CUP (6 OUNCES) SEMI-SWEET CHOCOLATE MORSELS

Heat oven to 350 degrees. Grease a 9- by 13-inch baking dish.

Melt chocolate and butter in a small saucepan over low heat or in the microwave on medium, stirring often. Stir until smooth and cool slightly.

Beat eggs in a medium bowl until well blended but not real foamy. Add sugar gradually and beat on low. Too much foam makes a crisp top on cooked brownies. Stir in vanilla. Stir in chocolate mixture, then stir in flour. Add nuts and chips and stir to blend. Pour into pan and bake 25 minutes. Brownies may seem just a little undercooked in the middle (not sloshy). Remove from the oven and cool completely before slicing into squares. Makes 24 brownies. They freeze beautifully.

## FRIDAY EVENING

KAREN'S SLOPPY JOES

For a trip down memory lane, make sloppy Joes. My friend Karen made these through the years of teenagers in her house. You've probably forgotten how good they taste and how easy they are to make. Make a bunch of filling and freeze it ahead.

1 1/2 POUNDS LEAN GROUND BEEF

2 TABLESPOONS BUTTER

1 LARGE ONION, CHOPPED

1 GREEN PEPPER, DICED

1 1/2 CUPS KETCHUP

2 TABLESPOONS BROWN SUGAR

2 TABLESPOONS PREPARED (BALLPARK) MUSTARD

1 TABLESPOON WORCESTERSHIRE SAUCE

SALT AND BLACK PEPPER (FRESHLY GROUND), TO TASTE.

Brown the beef in a wide, deep skillet. Set aside in a strainer or on paper towels to drain.

In the skillet, melt the butter. Add onion and bell pepper and cook over medium-low heat until soft and the onion is browning, about 10 minutes. Stir occasionally and adjust the heat if the vegetables appear to be burning.

Add remaining ingredients, including beef and 3/4 cup water. Cover the skillet and cook on low heat for 30 minutes. If mixture gets too dry, add a little water or sweet pickle brine to thin the sauce (the sweet pickle brine makes it more sloppy Joe-ish). Add salt and pepper to taste. Serve on buns.

Serves 8 or more.

## PORTOBELO SANDWICH WITH ZESTY RED ONION JAM

2 MEDIUM RED ONIONS

3 TABLESPOONS VEGETABLE OIL

2 TEASPOONS SOY SAUCE

2 TABLESPOONS BROWN SUGAR

1 TABLESPOON VINEGAR

1/4 TEASPOON CRUSHED RED PEPPER FLAKES

2 PORTOBELO MUSHROOM CAPS, ABOUT 3 OUNCES EACH

SALT AND (FRESHLY GROUND) BLACK PEPPER

1 JAR (8 TO 12 OUNCES) PEELED RED PEPPERS

1 LONG LOAF FAIRLY SOFT FRENCH OR ITALIAN BREAD (ABOUT 1 POUND), OR
    SUBSTITUTE HOAGIE-TYPE BUNS

6 OUNCES GOOD-QUALITY PROVOLONE OR CHEDDAR CHEESE

Peel the onions and slice them 1/4-inch thick. Heat 1 tablespoon of vegetable oil over high heat in a wide skillet and add the onions. Lower heat to medium and cook, stirring occasionally, until the onions are quite limp and beginning to brown, about 15 minutes. Add the soy sauce, sugar, vinegar and crushed red pepper flakes. Cook another 5 minutes, until the liquid has evaporated and the onions are coated with the mixture.

Meanwhile, heat the broiler. Place the portobelo caps on a lightly greased broiler pan and brush on both sides with remaining oil. Season generously with salt and pepper. Broil about 5 minutes on each side.

Remove peppers from jar and drain them briefly. Slice the bread horizontally, then in 4 pieces vertically. When the mushrooms come out of the broiler, slice them vertically about 1/4-inch thick. Divide the onion mixture among the sandwiches, then the mushrooms, then the red pepper slices. Top with cheese. Close the sandwiches and heat briefly if desired. Makes 4 sandwiches.

May be wrapped tightly in plastic wrap and refrigerated a day or two.

**ORZO SALAD**

This salad is reminiscent of tabbouleh—the parsley acts almost like a salad green. You can make this several days ahead and keep it covered and refrigerated.

1 POUND ORZO PASTA (SUBSTITUTE LARGE COUSCOUS SUCH AS ISRAELI)

1 TABLESPOON SALT

1 BUNCH PARSLEY

1/4 CUP CHOPPED MINT

1 BUNCH GREEN ONIONS

1 PINT CHERRY TOMATOES

1/2 CUP CURRANTS OR RAISINS

DRESSING:

1/3 CUP OLIVE OIL

2 TABLESPOONS VINEGAR, ANY KIND

1 TEASPOON DRIED OREGANO, OR 1 TABLESPOON FRESH (OPTIONAL)

1 TEASPOON SALT

1/2 TEASPOON (FRESHLY GROUND) BLACK PEPPER

Bring a large pot of water to boil. Add orzo and salt and cook until pasta is tender, 9 or so minutes.

Meanwhile, remove the toughest stems of the parsley (just whack them off at the most obvious place) and mince the parsley as finely as possible. Place in a large bowl as you do. Add chopped mint. Trim and mince green onions and place them in the bowl. Quarter cherry tomatoes and add them to the bowl. Add currants.

In a small bowl or jar, combine dressing ingredients and mix until salt dissolves. When the orzo is tender, drain it well and rinse with cold water. Drain well and add to bowl. Drizzle with dressing and stir to combine.

Serves 10 to 12.

SUGAR SNAP PEA SALAD

It may be that you have plenty of leftover coleslaw and you don't need more vegetables. But if you do, try this mixture of spring produce.

2 TABLESPOONS OLIVE OIL

1 TABLESPOON VINEGAR, PREFERABLY RASPBERRY OR APPLE

1 TEASPOON SUGAR

1/2 TEASPOON SALT

BLACK PEPPER TO TASTE

2 PINTS STRAWBERRIES

8 OUNCES SUGAR SNAP PEAS

Combine olive oil, vinegar, sugar, salt, and pepper in a blender. Hull 4 or 5 strawberries and add them to the blender. Blend until smooth. Remove strings from peas (if any, some varieties have strings, others don't). Cut the snap peas in half to make shorter snap peas. Hull strawberries and slice them thinly. Combine all ingredients in a bowl. Serves 8.

PEANUT BUTTER CHOCOLATE CHIP OATMEAL COOKIES

1/2 CUP BUTTER

1 1/4 CUPS PEANUT BUTTER

1 CUP LIGHT BROWN SUGAR

1 CUP SUGAR

3 EGGS

1 CUP ALL-PURPOSE FLOUR

1 TEASPOON BAKING SODA

3 CUPS ROLLED OATS (QUICK-COOKING OR OLD-FASHIONED)

12 OUNCES SEMISWEET CHOCOLATE MINI-CHIPS (OR CHIPS OF CHOICE)

Heat oven to 350 degrees. Beat butter and peanut butter together until fluffy and well-blended. Add sugars and beat well. Add eggs and beat well to combine. Add flour and baking soda. Stir into batter until evenly blended. Add chips and oats. Stir to combine evenly. Drop by tablespoons onto ungreased cookie sheets. Bake 12 minutes—they may look soft but shouldn't be shiny. Remove from cookie sheet and cool on rack. Makes about 3 dozen.

## CHICKEN TETRAZZINI

Tetrazzini sounds fancy but it's nothing more than chicken and mushrooms stirred into a cream sauce and poured over noodles. Nothing difficult about that. And it freezes beautifully. The 4 cups of chicken broth comes from 2 cans—if your cans are smaller than 16 ounces, just add a little water to make up the difference.

I often buy two turkey thighs to simmer and use in this dish, and I use the simmering broth as the liquid. You could also use store bought roast chicken, or other pre-cooked chicken.

SALT
1 POUND SPAGHETTI OR VERMICELLI
9 TABLESPOONS BUTTER OR VEGETABLE OIL
1 POUND SLICED MUSHROOMS
PEPPER, PREFERABLY FRESHLY GROUND
1 1/2 POUNDS (OR SO) COOKED CHICKEN OR TURKEY
1/2 CUP ALL-PURPOSE FLOUR
4 CUPS CHICKEN BROTH
1 CUP HEAVY (WHIPPING) CREAM
1/4 CUP SHERRY
1 1/2 TO 2 CUPS FRESHLY GRATED PARMESAN CHEESE
2 CUPS UNSEASONED BREAD CRUMBS

Heat oven to 350 degrees. Grease two 9- by 13-inch baking dishes (or dishes of similar size). Bring a large pot of water to a boil. Add 1 tablespoon of salt and noodles and cook until tender. Drain well and rinse with cold water.

In a wide, heavy skillet, melt 3 tablespoons butter over medium heat (or heat vegetable oil). Add mushrooms, increase heat to high, and cook until the mushrooms have reduced in size and all the liquid they give off is evaporated. Remove with slotted spoon to a large bowl. Cut chicken into pieces and add it to the mushrooms.

In the skillet, add remaining 6 tablespoons of butter and melt over medium heat. Add flour, a teaspoon of salt and lots of pepper, stirring to combine. Add chicken broth, whisking it in to smooth out lumps (If the chicken broth is hot, it goes into the flour much easier; if it is cold, the flour will seize up into a clump. That's O.K., just keep adding liquid a little at a time and keep stirring; it will loosen up.) Add the cream and sherry to the sauce and bring to a boil. Remove from heat and add 1 cup Parmesan cheese. Stir to incorporate. Combine sauce with mushrooms.

Divide noodles between 2 greased 9- by 13-inch casseroles then top with chicken mixture. Lift noodles to mix in the chicken and the sauce, combining as evenly as you can. Sprinkle remaining cheese and bread crumbs over the casseroles. Bake 25 to 30 minutes. Serves 12.

### PAN-FRIED HERBED CHERRY TOMATOES

I love recipes where you can just dump the ingredients in a pan. This one is that easy, and it's quick to make.

> 1/4 CUP OLIVE OIL
> 2 PINTS CHERRY TOMATOES
> 1 TEASPOON SALT
> 1/2 TEASPOON (FRESHLY GROUND) BLACK PEPPER
> 1 TEASPOON DRIED BASIL

Heat 2 tablespoons of olive oil in a wide, deep skillet over high heat. When the oil is hot, add a pint of tomatoes, half the salt, pepper and basil. Shake the pan and cook 2 minutes, or until they are warmed through. Pour into serving bowl and repeat with remaining tomatoes. Serve hot. Serves 10.

## STRAWBERRY FETA SPINACH SALAD

DRESSING:

    1/2 CUP SUGAR

    1/2 CUP VINEGAR

    1/2 CUP VEGETABLE OIL

    1/2 TEASPOON DRY MUSTARD

    1/2 TEASPOON SALT

    1/2 TEASPOON PAPRIKA

    1 CLOVE GARLIC, MINCED, ABOUT 1/2 TEASPOON

SALAD:

    1 PINT STRAWBERRIES

    8 OUNCES FETA CHEESE

    3 10-OUNCE BAGS READY-TO-EAT MIXED SALAD GREENS

Combine sugar, vinegar, oil, mustard, salt, paprika and garlic in a quart jar. Close tightly and shake to dissolve sugar (this keeps weeks in the refrigerator). Remove hulls and slice strawberries. Put salad greens in a large bowl and toss with dressing to taste. Sprinkle with strawberries and crumble feta over the top. Serves 10 to 12.

## CORN MUFFINS

Buttermilk really adds to the flavor of these muffins.

    1 1/2 CUPS CORNMEAL

    1/2 CUP FLOUR

    2 TEASPOONS BAKING POWDER

    1/2 TEASPOON BAKING SODA

    1 TEASPOON SALT

    2 EGGS

    1 1/2 CUPS BUTTERMILK

    3 TABLESPOONS MELTED BUTTER

    3/4 CUP CANNED CREAMED CORN

Heat oven to 425 degrees. Spray or lightly oil a 12-cup muffin tin. Combine dry ingredients and stir to mix. In a medium bowl, beat the eggs. Add buttermilk and beat again. Beat in butter and creamed corn. Stir in dry ingredients just to blend. Divide mixture among muffin cups and bake for 25 minutes, or until muffins have brown patches on top. Makes 12 muffins.

### BEST CARAMEL CAKE

In the South, a chocolate cake is a white cake with chocolate icing, and a caramel cake is a white (or yellow) cake with caramel icing. The old-fashioned caramel cake calls for a hard-cooked caramel icing—it's almost like candy. I like this version better. The icing is creamier and not as sweet as the candy icing.

### CAKE:

> 1 CUP UNSALTED BUTTER
> 2 CUPS SUGAR
> 3 CUPS SIFTED CAKE FLOUR
> 3 TEASPOONS BAKING POWDER
> 1 TEASPOON SALT
> 4 EGGS
> 1 CUP MILK
> 1 1/2 TEASPOONS VANILLA

### ICING:

> 1/2 CUP SUGAR
> 3 TABLESPOONS COLD WATER
> 8 OUNCES CREAM CHEESE
> 1 POUND (4 OR 5 CUPS) POWDERED SUGAR
> 1 TEASPOON VANILLA
> 1/4 TEASPOON SALT

To make the cake: Heat oven to 350 degrees. Grease and flour two 9-inch cake pans. Line with circles of waxed paper. Beat butter and gradually add sugar, beating until light and fluffy (about 8 minutes). Sift flour with baking powder and salt. Add eggs, 1 at a time, to butter mixture, beating well and scraping sides of bowl after each addition. Add flour mixture alternately with milk and vanilla, beating after each addition until smooth. Pour batter into prepared pans. Bake 25 to 30 minutes or until the cake springs back when pressed in the middle with a finger. Cool in pans 10 minutes. Remove from pans and finish cooling on racks.

To make the icing: Melt sugar in a small skillet or other pan over low or medium-low heat until it turns dark. Put water in a small dish and have it ready. The sugar will begin to brown on the outside edges of the pan. Swirl the pan on the burner to expose all the sugar to heat evenly and minimize the hot spots. Tip the pan if you must to prevent over-browning, but don't stir, that causes more problems than it's worth. When virtually all of the sugar is melted and the sugar is dark, add water all at once and move your hand quickly. Remove from heat and set aside to cool completely. Stir over low heat, if necessary, to dissolve sugar.

Beat cream cheese until soft and fluffy. Beat in 2 cups powdered sugar, a cup at a time, until it's incorporated. Add cooled caramel, vanilla and salt. Add remaining powdered sugar to achieve spreading consistency. Spread between layers and on surface and sides of cake.

Makes 1 cake that serves 12 to 16.

Best caramel cake, page 47

Derby club sandwich, page 50, with tuna salad, page 50, and chocolate cherry bars, page 51

Hot brown casserole, page 56

Bibb lettuce salad with blue cheese and pecans, page 61

Strawberries Derby, page 67

True grits, page 79

Favorite green bean salad, page 80

Chocolate chip pecan pie, page 81

Chicken salad with boiled dressing, page 88, with Sally Lunn, page 90

Bourbon ball torte, page 92

Mint juleps, page 93, with cheese coins, page 73

Kentucky burgoo, page 94

Benedictine, page 100

Asparagus dippers, page 103

Cheese torte, page 104

Turkey hash, page 108, on corn cakes, page 109

## SATURDAY BREAKFAST

### BACON FOR A CROWD
1 POUND BACON

Heat oven to 350 degrees. Place bacon slices on a shallow baking sheet so they fit in one layer. It's OK if they overlap a little. Bake 10 minutes. Remove from oven and drain. Flip the bacon and straighten them out, then place back in oven and cook 5 to 10 minutes more, or until cooked through. Drain bacon. Serves 8 to 10.

### FRENCH TOAST FOR A CROWD
4 EGGS
1 1/2 CUPS MILK
10 OR SO PIECES FRENCH-STYLE WHITE BREAD, CUT 1 1/2-INCHES THICK
1/4 CUP VEGETABLE OIL

Beat the eggs in a 9- by 13-inch or similar-size casserole. Add the milk and beat again until evenly blended. Put as much bread as you can in one layer. Once they are all in the pan, go back and flip them over gently. Cover the dish with plastic wrap and refrigerate overnight. Heat two large skillets over medium-high heat. Divide vegetable oil between them. When the oil is hot, add bread pieces to skillet. When bread is well-browned on one side, flip the pieces over. Turn heat to medium-low and let the pieces cook 15 minutes, flipping bread or changing temperature to create a nice browning on both sides. Serve with syrup or strawberry sauce. Serves 5 to 10.

### STRAWBERRY SAUCE
1 QUART STRAWBERRIES
1/2 CUP SUGAR
JUICE OF 1 LEMON
2 TABLESPOONS UNSALTED BUTTER

Remove tops from strawberries and cut the berries into pieces, putting them into a medium-size saucepan. Add sugar, lemon juice and butter. Cook over medium heat, stirring occasionally, until the sugar has dissolved and the mixture is a hot, pourable sauce. Serve with French toast. Also delicious with buttermilk pound cake and as an ice cream topping. Makes about 2 cups sauce.

## SATURDAY AT THE TRACK

DERBY CLUB SANDWICH

Be forgiving on the amounts of ingredients in this sandwich. If your slices of bread are large, you may want more bacon and chicken. If you want the dressing a little looser, add another tablespoon of mayonnaise.

1/4 CUP MAYONNAISE

1/2 CUP BLUE CHEESE

4 SLICES BACON

2 SKINLESS, BONELESS CHICKEN BREAST HALVES, ABOUT 10 OUNCES

1 HEAD LEAF LETTUCE OR ROMAINE

1 MEDIUM TOMATO

8 SLICES BREAD

Mix mayonnaise with blue cheese. Cut bacon in half to make short pieces and cook the pieces until the are crisp. Cook chicken in microwave, simmering water or in the skillet where you cooked the bacon until cooked through. Wash and dry lettuce. Slice tomato thinly. Spread 4 pieces of bread with mayonnaise. Top with lettuce, then tomato slice, 2 strips of bacon per piece of bread. Slice chicken as thinly as you can and place on top of bacon. Place bread on top of chicken and press down gently to smoosh all the ingredients together. Wrap tightly in plastic. Serves 4.

TUNA SALAD

15 RIPE, IMPORTED-STYLE OLIVES (SUCH AS KALAMATA)

2 HARD-COOKED EGGS (SEE NOTE)

2  6 1/2 TO 7-OUNCE CANS TUNA, DRAINED

2 RIBS CELERY, CHOPPED

2 TABLESPOONS SWEET PICKLE RELISH, OPTIONAL

1/2 CUP MAYONNAISE

2 TEASPOONS VINEGAR

1/4 TEASPOON SALT

1/4 TEASPOON (FRESHLY GROUND) BLACK PEPPER

Pit olives if necessary, slice them and put them in a bowl. Peel and chop hard-cooked eggs. Add them to olives. Add remaining ingredients to bowl and stir to mix. Serve as sandwich filling or simply as salad. Serves 4 to 6.

> Hard-cooked eggs: Everyone has a method, and here's mine. I put cold eggs in a saucepan and cover them with cold water. I put the pan on high heat and bring the water to a boil, then cover the pan, remove from the heat and let them sit for 20 minutes.

## CHOCOLATE CHERRY BARS

1 CUP ALL-PURPOSE FLOUR

1/2 TEASPOON BAKING SODA

1/4 TEASPOON SALT

1/2 CUP PLUS 2 TABLESPOONS (1 1/4 STICKS) UNSALTED BUTTER, ROOM TEMPERATURE

1/2 CUP SUGAR

1/2 CUP (PACKED) DARK BROWN SUGAR

1 LARGE EGG

1/2 TEASPOON ALMOND EXTRACT

1 CUP OLD-FASHIONED OATS

1 1/2 CUPS SEMISWEET CHOCOLATE CHIPS

1 CUP DRIED TART CHERRIES OR CRANBERRIES

1/2 CUP SLIVERED ALMONDS, TOASTED

Grease a 9- by 13-inch baking pan. Heat oven to 350 degrees.

Combine flour, baking soda and salt into medium bowl. Using electric mixer, beat butter, sugar and brown sugar in large bowl until well blended. Mix in egg and almond extract. Beat in flour mixture. Mix in oats, then chocolate chips, cherries and almonds. Spread the mixture in the prepared pan and bake for 20 minutes. Cool 20 minutes before cutting. Makes 30 squares.

$$\boxed{\text{SATURDAY DINNER}}$$

PEPPER SAUSAGE AND CHICKEN

First you cook the meat, then you cook vegetables, then you cook them all together.

4 ITALIAN LINK SAUSAGES (ABOUT 1 POUND)
1/3 CUP OLIVE OIL
4 BONELESS, SKINLESS CHICKEN BREAST HALVES OR 8 THIGHS OR COMBINATION
SALT AND (FRESHLY GROUND) BLACK PEPPER
1 LARGE ONION
2 RED BELL PEPPERS
1 GREEN PEPPER
1 TEASPOON DRIED BASIL
1 TEASPOON DRIED OREGANO
1 CAN (14.5 TO 16 OUNCES) CRUSHED TOMATOES

Cut sausages in half to make shorter sausages. Heat 2 tablespoons of oil in a wide skillet over medium high heat and add sausages. If you've bought chicken breast, cut it in half to make 2 stubbier pieces. Sprinkle chicken with salt and pepper. If there's enough room in the pan for the chicken, add it, if not, remove the sausage when it has 2 browned stripes down either side. Add chicken and brown quickly on both sides (it doesn't have to cook through).

As sausage and chicken cook, peel onion and slice 1/4-inch thick. Stem and core peppers and cut in 2-inch (or so) cubes.

After removing chicken from skillet, add remaining oil and the onion slices and cook 5 minutes, stirring occasionally. The onion should brown some, if not, cook a little longer. Add peppers and cover. Cook 5 minutes more. Remove cover and add herbs, tomatoes and sausage. If you're using chicken thighs, add them also. Cover and cook 15 minutes. Add chicken breast pieces and cook 5 minutes more. Serves 8.

## CHEESY ZITI

1 POUND ZITI
1 TABLESPOON SALT
4 TABLESPOONS OLIVE OIL
3 TABLESPOONS FLOUR
2 TEASPOONS DRY MUSTARD
2 TEASPOONS WORCESTERSHIRE SAUCE
1/4 TEASPOON CAYENNE PEPPER
4 CUPS MILK
12 OUNCES EXTRA SHARP CHEDDAR CHEESE, GRATED (ABOUT 3 CUPS)
4 OUNCES PARMESAN OR ROMANO CHEESE, GRATED (ABOUT 1 CUP)

Grease a 9- by 13- casserole or pan of similar size. Bring a large pot of water to boil. Add ziti and 2 teaspoons salt. Cook according to package directions until barely tender. Heat olive oil in a medium-size saucepan over medium heat. Add flour, mustard, Worcestershire, cayenne pepper and remaining teaspoon of salt. Stir to blend. Add milk (this is easiest if it's hot) and stir or whisk constantly to smooth out the lumps. When all the milk has been added, bring to a boil, stirring. Remove from heat and stir in cheddar cheese and 1/2 cup of Parmesan cheese.

Combine drained noodles and cheese sauce and spoon into casserole. Sprinkle remaining cheese on top. You can refrigerate the mixture or bake at 350 degrees for 30 minutes or until mixture is bubbly around the edges. If it's cold from the refrigerator it will take longer to heat through. Serves 8 to 10.

## GARLIC BREAD

The bread may be prepared, wrapped tightly and frozen before cooking.

1 FRENCH OR ITALIAN-STYLE LOAF (1 POUND)
3 CLOVES GARLIC, ABOUT 1 1/2 TEASPOONS MINCED
1/2 CUP BUTTER OR OLIVE OIL

Heat broiler to high and put oven rack about 4 inches from the heat. Cut the bread in half lengthwise. Combine garlic and butter in a small bowl and moosh with a fork to mix them. Spread on cut surfaces of bread (use a pastry brush to brush olive oil on surfaces). Place bread on cookie sheet and slide under broiler. Watch carefully. Take the bread out when the surface browns. Cut each half in 4 pieces. Serves 8.

### BEST MUSTARD VINAIGRETTE

> 1 CUP OLIVE OIL
> 1/4 CUP VINEGAR
> 1 TABLESPOON DIJON-STYLE MUSTARD
> 2 TEASPOONS SALT
> 1 TEASPOON SUGAR
> 1/2 TO 1 TEASPOON PEPPER, PREFERABLY FRESHLY GROUND

Combine all ingredients in a jar with a tight-fitting lid. Shake until sugar and salt dissolve. Makes about 1 1/4 cups. Keeps forever in the refrigerator. Use on tossed salads, for marinating meat, to brush on vegetables before grilling, etc.

### MARY'S CHOCOLATE PIE

This is one of my favorite dessert recipes—easy and popular. Some people have told me that their filling mixture is too much for their pie pan. If that happens to you, just discard what doesn't seem to fit. This pie will puff a little, then fall when it comes out of the oven.

A recipe for pastry follows, but if you've perfected one, that's the one to stick with. Or buy a crust if you're more comfortable with that.

> 3 OUNCES (SQUARES) UNSWEETENED CHOCOLATE
> 1/2 CUP BUTTER
> 4 EGGS
> 3 TABLESPOONS LIGHT CORN SYRUP
> 1 1/2 CUPS SUGAR
> 1 TEASPOON VANILLA
> 1/4 TEASPOON SALT
> 1 UNCOOKED 9-INCH PIE CRUST

Combine chocolate and butter in a small saucepan set in a larger saucepan of hot water, or in a microwave-safe dish. Heat gently to melt chocolate, stirring often to combine evenly. Set aside to cool.

Heat oven to 350 degrees. Beat eggs in a large bowl until they are completely blended but not too foamy. Beat in corn syrup. Add sugar slowly as you continue to beat on low speed, then stir in vanilla and salt. Stir in cooled chocolate. Pour into pie crust and bake 35 minutes or until set. It can seem a little soft in the middle, but not jiggle-y. Serves 8 to 10. This is especially delicious served warm with cold unsweetened whipped cream.

## ONE-CRUST PIE PASTRY

> 1 CUP ALL-PURPOSE FLOUR
> 1/2 TEASPOON SALT
> 1/3 CUP CHILLED SHORTENING
> 1 TABLESPOON COLD BUTTER
> 2 TO 3 TABLESPOONS WATER

Combine the flour and salt in a medium-size bowl. Add half the shortening and use a pastry blender or two knives to cut it into the flour until it resembles coarse meal. Add remaining shortening and the butter and cut until the largest pieces are the size of small peas. Add water and stir to combine. You should be able to gather the dough in a ball. If you need to add a little more water, do so, a couple of teaspoons should do it. Use a rolling pin and roll the dough on a lightly-floured surface or on a piece of plastic wrap to about 10 1/2-inches in diameter, or large enough to fill your pie pan. Press gently into pan and trim edges. Chill or freeze until needed. Makes 1 pie crust.

## SUNDAY BRUNCH

### HOT BROWN CASSEROLE

Louisville's Brown Hotel is given credit for inventing this recipe, but others pre-date it. Suffice to say that the Brown named the sandwich, which normally consists of sliced turkey on toast covered with a cream sauce that's been augmented with a hefty dose of sharp cheddar cheese, topped with bacon and sometimes tomatoes. The recipes around town differ widely. At the Brown, they assemble it in single servings.

3/4 CUP BUTTER

3/4 CUP FLOUR

2 EGGS

6 CUPS MILK

2 CUPS GRATED EXTRA-SHARP CHEDDAR CHEESE, SUCH AS NEW YORK STATE

1/4 CUP HEAVY (WHIPPING) CREAM

SALT AND (FRESHLY GROUND) BLACK PEPPER, TO TASTE

16 SLICES WHITE BREAD, SUCH AS PEPPERIDGE FARM

16 THIN SLICES ROAST TURKEY

1/2 CUP FRESHLY GRATED PARMESAN CHEESE

PAPRIKA

8 BACON SLICES

1 CUP TOMATO, SEEDED AND DICED

Heat oven to 350 degrees.

In a large saucepan, melt butter. Add flour, stirring to make a roux. Cook 2 to 3 minutes. Thoroughly beat eggs. Beat into milk. While stirring, very slowly add milk mixture to butter mixture. Use a whisk and stir constantly to keep the flour from lumping (it may seize into a clump at first, just keep adding a little milk and stirring, it will loosen up). Bring the mixture to a boil over medium-high heat. Remove from heat and add cheddar cheese. Stir to melt, then add cream, salt and pepper to taste.

Toast bread in a toaster or place under broiler until golden on both sides. Line the bottom of a 9- by 13- by 2-inch casserole (6 slices) and an 8- by 8- by 2-inch (2 slices) with bread. Trim crust as necessary to make them fit, or use one large casserole dish if you have it. Cut the crust off the remaining slices and cut them in half on the diagonal to make triangles.  Top toast in casseroles with slices of turkey. Cover turkey with sauce. Sprinkle with Parmesan cheese and paprika. Place in oven for 15 minutes or until golden brown. While casserole is baking, cook bacon. Cut it in half to make 2 shorter strips and fry until crisp. Remove to absorbent toweling and drain. Core and halve tomato and scoop out seeds. Dice the tomato into small bits.

Remove the casserole(s) from the oven, sprinkle with tomato bits and cross 2 short pieces of bacon over each sandwich. Surround with toast points. Serves 8. Serve with salad.

### BOURBON BUTTERMILK PIE
CRUST:

> 1 CUP ALL-PURPOSE FLOUR
>
> 6 TABLESPOONS BUTTER, CUT INTO AT LEAST 8 PIECES
>
> 1/2 TEASPOON SALT
>
> 1 EGG

FILLING:

> 3 EGGS
>
> 1 1/4 CUPS SUGAR
>
> 1/2 CUP BUTTER, MELTED
>
> 2 TABLESPOONS ALL-PURPOSE FLOUR
>
> 1 CUP BUTTERMILK
>
> 1/4 CUP BOURBON (OR SUBSTITUTE 2 TEASPOONS VANILLA)
>
> 1/4 TEASPOON SALT

Crust: Combine flour, butter and salt in a medium-sized bowl. Use a pastry cutter or 2 knives to cut the butter into flour until the mixture resembles coarse meal. In a small bowl, beat egg and 1 tablespoon water together. Stir into flour mixture until well combined, then press the mixture together with your hands to form a ball. Flatten the ball into a disk 1 inch thick, wrap in plastic and refrigerate. For easiest rolling, let the dough chill 30 minutes. Roll to about 1/8-inch thickness and press into a 9-inch pie plate. Heat oven to 400 degrees. Spray the dull side of aluminum foil with non-stick cooking spray. Put the sprayed side down and press the foil flat against the pie crust. Fill the crust with dry beans, rice or aluminum pie weights and bake 20 minutes, or until the pie crust is set. Remove the beans and the foil (you can use the beans in cooking).

Filling: Beat eggs in a medium-sized bowl. Add sugar and butter and beat to blend. Beat in remaining ingredients. Pour into pie crust and place in the oven. Reduce oven temperature to 350 degrees and bake 40 minutes. The pie should be puffed in the center and will fall when it cools. Cool. Serves 8. Serve with fresh strawberries.

# FRIDAY–OAKS DAY

In Louisville, the day of the Kentucky Oaks may be the biggest food day of the entire festival, and certainly one of the biggest restaurant days of the year. Everyone who is coming into town is here, and all of them need feeding.

How they are fed differs with the occasion, of course. This may be the fanciest of all dinner parties, or it may be a cocktail party to introduce business clients to staff or out-of-town friends to neighbors. Then again, it might be most practical to have a casual, comfortable dinner with a few traditional dishes. There are Derby foods to fit any need.

## OAKS DINNER (FANCY)
Bibb lettuce with blue cheese and pecans
Beef tenderloin with Henry Bain sauce
Thelma's rolls
Roast asparagus
Corn pudding
Strawberries Derby
Louisville shortbread

## COCKTAIL PARTY
Sangria
Kentucky mint julep
Asian beef tenderloin
Pickled shrimp
Smoked trout horseradish dip
Cheese coins
Stuffed mushrooms (with country ham)
Caviar cucumbers
Chocolate chess bars

## OAKS DINNER (NOT FANCY)
Sun dried tomato spread
Barbecue chicken
True grits
Favorite green bean salad
Chocolate chip pecan pie

## OAKS DINNER (FANCY)

BIBB LETTUCE SALAD WITH BLUE CHEESE AND PECANS

Friends from out of town should be treated to Bibb lettuce salad at least once during their Derby stay. The small heads with soft, delicate leaves in waves of green to white were once popular in fine-dining establishments and had a national reputation as a fancy alternative to crunchy iceberg. The variety actually began with the experiments of gardener and War of 1812 veteran Maj. Jack Bibb, in his Frankfort, Kentucky, greenhouse. For the rest of us, it's a nice change from baby mixed greens.

4 HEADS BIBB LETTUCE
2 OUNCES (ABOUT 1/2 CUP) PECAN PIECES
4 OUNCES BLUE CHEESE
1/2 RED BELL PEPPER
1/2 CUP OLIVE OIL
2 TABLESPOONS RED WINE VINEGAR, OR VINEGAR OF CHOICE
1/2 TEASPOON SALT

Separate leaves of Bibb, then rinse and wrap in toweling to dry the leaves (you may put the towel-enclosed leaves in a plastic bag and hold them for a day or two). Toast pecan pieces in the microwave, toaster oven or conventional oven until they smell toasty and are golden brown. Chop into small bits. Crumble blue cheese. Dice red pepper into small bits.

Combine olive oil, vinegar and salt and stir or shake to dissolve salt. Toss dry lettuce leaves with dressing and arrange the leaves on 8 plates. Sprinkle with pecans, blue cheese and red peppers. Serves 8.

EASY BEEF TENDERLOIN

Nothing says elegance like beef tenderloin. Whether you're serving appetizers at a cocktail party or a sit-down dinner for 12, this boneless, easy-to-carve, tender meat earns its place as the easiest of entrees for cooks to prepare. That's why it's the unofficial Derby-week entree of choice. You might think it would be country ham, or fried chicken, or something distinctly Southern, but nope, it's tenderloin. If you're a once-a-year tenderloin cook, you'll need to review the basics:

• Whole beef tenderloin sold either trimmed or untrimmed, weighs from 4 to 7 pounds.
• Trimmed meat has had all fat and silverskin removed (silverskin is an inedible, tough membrane that can be removed from the meat with a sharp knife).
• Supermarket chains often feature special prices on whole, untrimmed beef tenderloin. It comes in the transparent, oxygen-free wrapper and the implication is that you will trim the meat yourself. Save yourself time and ask the meat cutter to trim it for you.
• If you end up trimming it, remove the thin outer membrane, the tough silverskin and fat deposits on the outside of the meat, including fat that runs the length of the tenderloin. Remove these fat deposits, and you'll have some loose, thin side pieces of meat flapping off the main roast, which need to be tied to the main part of the roast.
• You'll know you have a wonderful butcher if he ties the tenderloin together so it looks neat and cooks evenly. If the piece you buy seems to have a bigger middle and one or two loose sides, you may want to ask the meat cutter to tie it for you. Or you can tie it yourself at home. Even a crude tying with cotton string will help the meat cook more evenly and make it more attractive looking than letting the flaps hang loose. It doesn't need to look perfect when you tie it.
• Allow the meat to stand 10 minutes when it comes out of the oven. Cut the strings off and slice for serving.

Opinions differ on how long a roast should cook and at what temperature. A whole, trimmed tenderloin will cook to rare in about 30 minutes, if you cook it by the high-heat method (start it at 500 degrees, then lower the heat to 400). It will take an hour if you cook it at 350 degrees. Tenderloin roasts cook in the same amount of time, no matter what they weigh. That means a roast that's 6 inches long will cook in about the same time as an 18-inch roast.

Using a meat thermometer is the best way to ensure the meat is cooked to the desired doneness. In a pinch, you can cut into the meat to check its color.

Because even "inexpensive" beef tenderloin is an expensive cut, you don't want to overcook it. Now may be the time to buy a meat thermometer from your favorite cookware store, department store or supermarket, and use it.

The beef tenderloin has no fat marbling to speak of, so it will be extremely tough and dried out if you cook it all the way through. If you want to prepare meat to the well-done stage, it's best to choose a less expensive meat, such as sirloin tip.

Beef tenderloin tapers at the end, so the "butt end," or widest part, can be rare while the tail end is less so. If you want the whole roast to cook evenly, turn the thin end under and tie it so the roast has a uniform thickness.

You can increase the size of the tenderloin in the recipe below without adjusting the time you need to cook it. If you use a larger piece of meat, increase the seasonings (and make more pan sauce). The thyme and garlic are optional. What's important is the roasting technique—use it whenever you need pre-cooked beef tenderloin (for salads or hors d'oeuvres), or if you're roasting a tenderloin for dinner.

2 1/2 TO 3 POUNDS BEEF TENDERLOIN
1 TEASPOON CHOPPED FRESH THYME OR 1/2 TEASPOON DRIED
4 CLOVES FRESH GARLIC, MINCED, ABOUT 2 TEASPOONS
1 TEASPOON SALT
1/2 TEASPOON (FRESHLY GROUND) BLACK PEPPER
1 TABLESPOON OLIVE OIL

Remove the meat from the refrigerator an hour before cooking.

Heat the oven to 500 degrees. Combine thyme, garlic, salt and pepper. Brush the meat with olive oil. Rub the seasoning mixture all over the meat. Place on a roasting pan, put the pan in the oven, shut the door and immediately reduce heat to 400 degrees.

Roast the beef 30 minutes and read its internal temperature. At 125 degrees, its center will be red and slightly warm. At 135, the center will be pink.

Remove from oven, drape loosely with a piece of foil and let the meat stand at least 10 minutes before trying to carve it. (Its internal temperature will rise a few degrees on standing.) Slice as desired for serving. Serves 8.

EASY PAN SAUCE FOR BEEF TENDERLOIN
  This is a thin, "au jus" style sauce.

  PAN DRIPPINGS FROM BEEF TENDERLOIN
  1/2 CUP RED WINE
  1 CUP BEEF BROTH (PREFERABLY HOMEMADE)
  SALT AND PEPPER, TO TASTE
  3 TABLESPOONS BUTTER

  After roasting, remove beef from the pan. Pour any excess fat from the bottom
of the pan but don't scrape. Place the pan over low heat on top of the stove. Add wine
and stir to remove the browned bits on the pan. When the wine boils down to a
tablespoon or two, add beef broth. Add salt and pepper to taste, adjusting for less salt
if you're using a processed broth or concentrate of some kind. Simmer the mixture
until it measures about 3/4 cup. Cut butter in 3 or 4 pieces. Add it to the pan. Remove
from heat. Stir sauce rapidly with a fork or whisk to beat in the butter. Spoon sauce
over individual servings of cooked beef.

HENRY BAIN SAUCE
  Henry Bain sauce is a sweet-sour-spicy beef sauce invented by a maitre d' at
Louisville's then-all-male Pendennis Club in the early 20th century. It is Louisville's
standard steak sauce.

  1 (17-OUNCE) JAR MAJOR GREY'S CHUTNEY
  HALF OF A 9-OUNCE JAR IMPORTED OF PICKLED WALNUTS (OPTIONAL, SEE NOTE)
  1 (14-OUNCE) BOTTLE KETCHUP
  1 (11-OUNCE) BOTTLE A-1 STEAK SAUCE
  1 (10-OUNCE) BOTTLE WORCESTERSHIRE SAUCE
  1 (12-OUNCE) BOTTLE CHILI SAUCE
  TABASCO, TO TASTE

  Put the chutney and walnuts, if using, in a blender and chop fine or puree as you
prefer (you'll need to stop and stir). Combine with other ingredients and season to taste
with Tabasco. Makes 4 pints that keep forever, refrigerated. Serve with hot or cold roast
beef. Also good served with cream cheese as a cracker spread. Note: Pickled walnuts are
recommended in the Henry Bain sauce recipe in "The Farmington Cookbook," but not
in recipes written by former Louisville food writers Cissy Gregg and Marion Flexner.

## THELMA'S ROLLS

Making yeast rolls isn't for everybody, but hot bread is a sure sign of Southern hospitality and these rolls in particular are special. Thelma Clay Linton—caterer of choice in Harrodsburg for the better part of a century—had her recipe immortalized in Susanna Thomas' book, "Thelma's Treasures, The Secret Recipes of The Best Cook in Harrodsburg." In that book, Thomas passed on Thelma's advice for technique: "When you stir the yeast up with the warm water it should bubble up. If it don't, somethin's not right. When you roll your dough out, don't go over it back and forth, that does somethin' to it. You got to roll from the center out in one direction all the way around until your dough is about a half inch thick."

The original recipe makes 17 to 18 dozen. Here is the recipe halved. Leftovers can be frozen and reheated wrapped in foil in a 300-degree oven. My family heats them for breakfast. Or make bread pudding with them.

PINCH SUGAR
1 CUP WARM WATER
2 PACKAGES FAST-ACTING YEAST (ABOUT 4 TEASPOONS)
2 EGGS
1/2 CUP BUTTER
1/2 CUP CRISCO VEGETABLE SHORTENING
1 TEASPOON SALT
1 SCANT CUP SUGAR
1 CUP BOILING WATER
8 CUPS WHITE LILY ALL-PURPOSE FLOUR
1/2 TO 1 CUP MELTED BUTTER

Put a pinch of sugar in a bowl. Heat the cup of warm water to about 110 degrees. Pour it in the bowl. Add the yeast and stir for approximately 1 minute until the yeast is dissolved and bubbles.

In another bowl, put in the eggs and beat them with a mixer until stiff, approximately 5 minutes. In another bowl, beat the butter, Crisco, salt and sugar on medium until the mixture gets really creamy, about 3 to 5 minutes. Turn the mixer to low speed and add the boiling water. When that is mixed in, turn the mixer back up slightly and add the beaten eggs. When that is well mixed, add the yeast, turn up the mixer a little more and mix for 30 seconds to 1 minute.

Spread out a piece of wax paper or aluminum foil and sift the flour onto it.

continued...

Measure out 2 cups, add to the yeast mixture and mix by hand vigorously for 2 minutes until the flour is well blended. Add the rest of the flour 2 cups at a time, beating vigorously by hand for 2 minutes or so after each addition.

When all the flour is mixed in, beat the dough well by hand, scraping it up from the bottom of the bowl with a spatula while rotating the bowl. Brush the top of the dough with softened or melted butter or margarine. Cover the bowl well with foil and let sit several hours until the dough has doubled in size. Put in the refrigerator overnight.

When ready to bake, melt 1/2 to 1 cup butter or margarine in a saucepan and set aside.

Take out about a fourth of the dough and knead it with as little flour as possible. Don't bear down on the bread. Knead it gently and quickly. Roll it out 1/2-inch thick and cut with a biscuit cutter. Grease the bottom of a pan with melted butter. Dip each roll in the melted butter and place in the pan so it lightly touches the other rolls. Roll out the rest of the dough. Let the rolls sit in the pans about 3 hours while they rise.

Bake at 375 degrees for 15 minutes.

Makes about 8 dozen, depending on the activity of the yeast, the thickness of the dough and the size of the biscuit cutter.

### ROASTED ASPARAGUS

Oven roasting is a great way to prepare vegetables—no less so asparagus. This dish is quite good at room temperature. Before serving, you may drizzle with additional olive oil and balsamic vinegar, if desired.

75 MEDIUM ASPARAGUS SPEARS (ABOUT 4 OR 5 BUNCHES), TRIMMED OF TOUGH ENDS
1/2 CUP GOOD-QUALITY OLIVE OIL
SALT (PREFERABLY KOSHER SALT) AND FRESHLY GROUND PEPPER TO TASTE

Heat oven to 400 degrees. Lay asparagus on cookie sheets in a single layer. Drizzle with olive oil, making sure the tips are well coated. Sprinkle with salt and pepper.

Cook for 15 minutes, or until the asparagus is tender, deep green and beginning to brown in places. Serves 12 or more.

## CORN PUDDING

This pudding tastes best when made with whole milk.

1/2 CUP FLOUR
1/2 CUP CORNMEAL
2 TABLESPOONS SUGAR
1 TEASPOON SALT
6 TABLESPOONS BUTTER, MELTED
3 10-OUNCE PACKAGES FROZEN CORN
6 EGGS
6 CUPS MILK

Combine flour, cornmeal, sugar and salt in a large bowl. Mix in the butter and corn. Beat eggs well. Add milk, then stir into corn mixture. Pour into a 4-quart, greased casserole, or 2 smaller casseroles.

At this point, it may be refrigerated overnight or frozen for several weeks. (If you are freezing, use a dish that is freezer- and oven-safe.)

To serve, thaw and bake in a 400-degree oven 40 to 50 minutes, stirring every 10 minutes for the first 30 minutes. Pudding should be soft but set in center when done and top should be golden.) Serves 12.

## STRAWBERRIES DERBY

Think of strawberries Romanoff with a touch of bourbon added. In truth, you can use any distinctive liquor to flavor this sauce—Grand Marnier would give it a lovely orange flavor. The sauce can be made 3 or 4 days in advance of when you need it. Cover it well for storage.

2 QUARTS FRESH STRAWBERRIES
1 QUART SOUR CREAM
1 CUP BROWN SUGAR
1 TABLESPOON VANILLA
2 TABLESPOONS BOURBON

Wash berries. Pinch off their hulls and place berries on absorbent toweling. Combine sour cream, brown sugar, vanilla and bourbon. Stir to dissolve sugar. Divide strawberries among 8 dessert bowls. Spoon sauce over fruit. Serves 8. Pass sugar cookies or shortbread.

LOUISVILLE SHORTBREAD

Cooks are often confused by the virtues of salted butter versus unsalted butter. What to use when? Unsalted butter—sometimes referred to as "sweet" butter—is more than butter without salt. Unsalted butter has what some cooks call a more "lactic" taste. It tastes sweeter.

Unsalted butter is best when baking buttery sweets—shortbread, for instance. The fresh, buttery flavor is the highlight in this not-too-sweet crumbly cookie.

1 CUP UNSALTED BUTTER
1 CUP LIGHT BROWN SUGAR
1 EGG, SEPARATED
1/2 TEASPOON SALT
1/2 TEASPOON FRESHLY GRATED LEMON RIND, OPTIONAL
2 CUPS ALL-PURPOSE FLOUR

Heat oven to 325 degrees. Beat the butter until creamy. Add the brown sugar and egg yolk and beat well to combine evenly. The mixture should be light. Stir in salt and lemon rind if using. Add flour a little at a time and mix in with a long spoon until the mixture is evenly blended. Pat into a 9- by 9-inch baking pan. Beat egg white until it's just foamy and no longer stringy. Brush the top of the shortbread with it. Prick the shortbread in parallel lines using the tines of a fork (do this quickly, don't be real obsessive about it). Bake for 35 minutes or until barely brown. Remove from oven and, while the shortbread is hot, cut it into fingers about 3 inches long and 1 inch wide. Remove from pan when cool. Makes about 27 fingers.

## COCKTAIL PARTY

### SANGRIA

My sangria makes a great addition to cocktail parties because it's festive, delicious and relatively low in alcohol—more like a wine spritzer. Serve it in a glass pitcher, if you have one, with fruit slices floating in it, and keep an ice bucket nearby.

The proportion of sweetened fruit juice is highly variable and really a matter of taste. I don't like mine too fruity, but just like to flavor the wine a little. Likewise, add as much seltzer as you think is reasonable. I tend to add about equal parts wine and seltzer, but you may prefer something different. Chill all ingredients before mixing. Wine and fruit can be mixed ahead but seltzer should be added at the last minute.

2/3 CUP FRESH LIME JUICE
2/3 CUP SUGAR
2 OR 3 BOTTLES (750 ML.) WINE, RED OR WHITE
1 TO 2 LITERS UNFLAVORED SELTZER OR SODA WATER

Combine lime juice and sugar and shake to dissolve sugar. Add 1/4 cup to a large pitcher. Add a bottle of wine and stir to blend. Add a liter of seltzer. The entire recipe makes enough to serve at least 12. Serve over ice or cold in stemmed glasses.

### Kentucky mint julep

The point of a mint julep is to barely season bourbon with a little fresh mint. Mint is sometimes growing in local gardens at Derby time and with any luck you can be lavish with both it and your bourbon. Remember, this is a cold, bold drink with a light mint essence, not a minty sweet drink that has been spiked with some anonymous liquor. For directions on making mint juleps in bulk, check our Derby Day pot luck menu, page 93.

2 sprigs fresh mint
1 teaspoon sugar
Crushed ice
2 jiggers Kentucky bourbon
Additional mint sprigs for garnish

Remove leaves from mint and put them in the bottom of a silver julep cup or glass. Add sugar and bruise the leaves with the sugar using the end of a wooden spoon or some other blunt implement. Add bourbon and stir, then add ice to fill the cup.

To serve, insert a straw through the ice and garnish the drink with more mint. These sprigs should be the same height as the straw, so the nose of the imbiber draws in the bouquet of the mint. Serves 1.

### Asian beef tenderloin

Thinly sliced beef tenderloin makes perfect hors d'oeuvres for the same reason it makes a perfect entree—it's easy for the cook and pleases nearly everyone. I know people who buy other hors d'oeuvres from a caterer and cook the beef themselves. You can, of course, cook the tenderloin in the preceding menu, chill it, cut it thinly and serve it with thin slices of baguette. Or you can do something different. I happen to love this, with its incendiary wasabi and the Asian flavors of soy sauce and ginger.

2 pounds beef tenderloin, trimmed of fat and silverskin
2 tablespoons soy sauce
1 tablespoon rice wine
1 tablespoon fresh lemon juice
2 tablespoons fresh grated or minced ginger
3 large cloves garlic, minced fine or put through a press
1 green onion, thinly sliced
Salt and (freshly ground) black pepper
1 cup good quality mayonnaise
1 tablespoon wasabi paste, or to taste
Lettuce leaves, French bread, rice crackers, etc.
3 tablespoons toasted sesame seeds

Remove the meat from the refrigerator 1 hour before cooking.

Heat oven to 500 degrees. Place meat on a roasting pan. Place in the oven, reduce heat to 400 and cook until the internal temperature reads 140 degrees (about 40 minutes) for medium-rare. Remove from the oven. Let cool.

In a large plastic zipper-style bag, combine soy sauce, rice wine, lemon juice, ginger, garlic, and onion. Add salt and pepper. Place cooled meat in soy-sauce mixture and let it marinate several hours or overnight, turning often.

Pat meat dry and cut in very thin slices.

Mix mayonnaise and wasabi paste. Place a slice of beef on a lettuce leaf, top with a dab of wasabi mayonnaise and sprinkle with sesame seeds, or thinly slice French bread (or your choice of edible holder), spread with mayonnaise, top with beef and sprinkle with sesame. Or place meat on a cracker, add a dab of mayonnaise, and sprinkle with sesame seeds.

Or put ultra-thin slices of beef on a platter and scatter sesame seeds over the top. Serve with wasabi mayonnaise, thinly sliced French bread and/or lettuce leaves.

Makes about 60 hors d'oeuvres.

## Pickled shrimp

An old-fashioned dish with lots of flair.

2 CUPS APPLE CIDER VINEGAR
1/2 CUP MIXED PICKLING SPICES
2 TEASPOONS SALT
1 TEASPOON BLACK PEPPERCORNS
1 INCH FRESH GINGER, PEELED
1/2 TEASPOON DRY MUSTARD
1 MEDIUM RED ONION
1 LEMON
3 POUNDS COOKED, PEELED LARGE SHRIMP
4 BAY LEAVES
1 1/2 CUPS OLIVE OIL

Combine vinegar, pickling spices, salt, peppercorns, ginger, and dry mustard in a non-reactive saucepan such as stainless steel or enamel-coated (iron or aluminum will react with the vinegar). Bring to a boil over high heat, reduce heat and simmer 5 minutes. Remove from heat and set aside to cool.

Slice the onion and lemon thinly. Scatter the slices in the bottom of a serving bowl (glass is lovely). Top with shrimp. Add bay leaves. Pour olive oil over all.

When the vinegar is cool, pour it through a strainer into the shrimp bowl. Shake the bowl to settle the shrimp into the vinegar mixture. If the liquid doesn't cover the shrimp, add a little water. Cover and chill at least overnight. The shrimp keeps up to 2 weeks in the refrigerator.

Serve cold. Three pounds of shrimp will serve 12 people when served with other cocktail food.

## Smoked trout dip

You might not expect it, but Kentucky is a land of trout. Successful trout farms have grown up in the region as the number of tobacco farms have diminished. In Louisville, a company called Shuckman's smokes Kentucky trout, and the product is available at finer groceries, some liquor stores and specialty stores around town. But of course, any smoked trout, or flaky smoked fish, will work in this recipe.

8 OUNCES CREAM CHEESE, SOFTENED
1/2 CUP SOUR CREAM, MORE OR LESS
8 OUNCES (OR SO) SMOKED TROUT, SKINNED IF NECESSARY AND FLAKED
2 GREEN ONIONS, TRIMMED AND MINCED
1 TABLESPOON HORSERADISH (OPTIONAL)
1/2 TEASPOON CAYENNE PEPPER

Beat cream cheese until no lumps remain. Beat in sour cream until smooth. Add remaining ingredients and stir. Serve with crackers. Serve as a dip with crackers or vegetables. Makes about 1 pint. Add more sour cream to make a thinner dip.


CHEESE COINS

It doesn't get more delicious than cheese coins. Unfortunately, they are tedious to make, which is why you see exorbitantly-priced packages of similar products in gourmet stores. The bought ones are fabulous, for the most part—what's not to like about cheese pastry, after all—but if you're up for making them, or assigning someone else to, this is a great recipe. It can be assembled quickly in a food processor.

1 CUP FLOUR
1/2 POUND (ABOUT 2 CUPS) GRATED EXTRA SHARP CHEDDAR CHEESE
1/2 CUP BUTTER
1/2 TEASPOON CAYENNE PEPPER
1/4 TEASPOON (FRESHLY GROUND) BLACK PEPPER
1/4 TEASPOON SALT

Combine flour, cheese, butter, cayenne, black pepper, and salt in a large bowl. Mix until smooth. Form into a roll about 1 1/2 inches in diameter. Wrap in foil or plastic wrap and freeze 2 or more hours. Slice into thin wafers (about 1/8-inch thick) and place very close together on an ungreased baking sheet. Bake in a 375-degree oven for 10 minutes, or until cooked through. Makes about 4 dozen wafers. The dough may be frozen for months. Keep the cooked discs in a tightly-covered container and they will also keep very well for weeks.

## Mushrooms stuffed with country ham

In the beginning, this started as a dish to use up bits and pieces of country ham left from carving. You wouldn't necessarily call for "4 ounces." But these days, the ham is available in a variety of forms, sometimes cooked and ready for slicing at the supermarket deli.

You need firm, white, pretty mushrooms for stuffing.

2 1/2 POUNDS MEDIUM MUSHROOMS
1/2 CUP OLIVE OIL
1 MEDIUM ONION
3 CLOVES GARLIC, MINCED, ABOUT 1 1/2 TEASPOONS
1/2 BUNCH FRESH PARSLEY
2 CUPS UNSEASONED DRY BREAD CRUMBS
4 OUNCES COUNTRY HAM, GROUND OR CHOPPED FINE
1 TEASPOON DRIED THYME

Remove the stems from mushrooms and chop them fine. Heat a wide skillet over medium heat. Add 1/4 cup olive oil and mushroom stems. As they cook, peel and mince the onion, adding it to the pan as you do. Add garlic. Remove large stems from parsley and mince the parsley. Add it to the skillet and stir, cooking until the parsley is wilted and the onion beginning to brown. Remove from heat and stir in bread crumbs, ham and thyme. Use mixture to stuff mushroom caps. Heat oven to 350 degrees. Arrange caps on a baking sheet. Drizzle with remaining 1/4 cup of olive oil. Bake 20 minutes. Serves 10 or so at a cocktail buffet.

## CAVIAR CUCUMBERS

In another life, these cucumber rounds might be topped with wasabi-flavored cream cheese and garnished with pickled ginger. But for Derby cocktails, we make them reminiscent of Benedictine. Red caviar is used for its beautiful color and intense flavor but you could just as easily use crumbled cooked bacon or chopped black olives (the imported kind, such as Kalamata).

Conventional supermarket cucumbers will work, but sometimes their waxy skins are just too tough. Of course you can peel them, or peel them partially so there are stripes of white flesh and green peel.

8 OUNCES CREAM CHEESE (LOW-FAT WILL WORK)

1/4 CUP SOUR CREAM OR HEAVY (WHIPPING) CREAM

1/2 BUNCH GREEN ONIONS (3 OR 4)

1/2 TEASPOON SALT

1/2 TEASPOON CAYENNE PEPPER

1 LONG ENGLISH CUCUMBER OR 2 REGULAR CUCUMBERS

1 SMALL JAR (4 OUNCES) RED CAVIAR, OR YOUR FAVORITE CAVIAR

Beat cream cheese until fluffy and no lumps remain. Add sour cream and beat to combine. Trim green onions of roots and wilted tops and trim within 3 inches of the white root. Mince the onion and add it to the cream cheese along with salt and cayenne pepper. Stir to combine. You may cover and refrigerate this mixture for several days.

When ready to serve, trim the cucumber and cut in 1/4-inch thick slices. Top with cream cheese mixture and then top with a little caviar. Refrigerate until serving. Serves about 12.

## CHOCOLATE CHESS BARS

CRUST:

>2 CUPS FLOUR
>
>1/2 CUP BUTTER, SOFTENED
>
>1/4 CUP SUGAR
>
>1/4 TEASPOON SALT

FILLING:

>2 OUNCES UNSWEETENED CHOCOLATE
>
>1/2 CUP BUTTER
>
>4 EGGS
>
>1 TABLESPOON BOURBON, OPTIONAL
>
>1 TEASPOON VANILLA
>
>1 1/4 CUP SUGAR
>
>2 TABLESPOONS ALL-PURPOSE FLOUR
>
>1/4 TEASPOON SALT

Heat oven to 325 degrees.

To make the crust: Mix flour, butter, sugar, and salt until evenly blended. Press into a 9- by 13-inch baking pan and bake for 20 minutes.

To make filling: Combine chocolate and butter in a bowl set over hot water or in a microwave-safe dish and melt with gentle heat, stirring often. Set aside.

Beat eggs to break them up, but don't get them too foamy. Beat in bourbon and vanilla. Stir together sugar, flour and salt and stir the mixture into the eggs. Stir in melted chocolate mixture. Pour into crust and bake for 35 minutes, or until the filling is set. Chill, then cut into bars. Makes 48 bars.

## OAKS DINNER (NOT FANCY)

### SUN-DRIED TOMATO SPREAD

This spread is easiest to make in a food processor. It can be done in a blender, but you must stop often and move the ingredients around.

> 1 1/2 CUPS DRIED TOMATOES (NOT THE KIND IN OIL), ABOUT 6 OUNCES
> 1 RED BELL PEPPER
> 1 CLOVE FRESH GARLIC, ABOUT 1/2 TEASPOON MINCED
> 2 TABLESPOONS VINEGAR
> 1/2 CUP OLIVE OIL
> PINCH RED PEPPER FLAKES
> 1/4 CUP CAPERS
> CHOPPED FRESH BASIL

Boil 1 cup water. Add dried tomatoes and let them stand 1 hour, turning them occasionally. Drain the tomatoes but reserve the water.

Chop up the tomatoes and put in the container of a food processor fitted with a steel blade or blender. Core and seed the red pepper, cut roughly into chunks and add to tomatoes along with garlic, vinegar and 1/4 cup tomato water. Process or blend, scraping down the container often, to make a smooth paste. Drizzle in olive oil as you process or blend, then the red pepper flakes.

Tomatoes come in different states of dryness and depending on how dry yours are they may need more moisture. I tend to move among the three choices—water, oil and vinegar trying not to make the mixture too tart but keeping a good balance of flavors. You want it an easy spreading consistency. Remove from container and stir in capers. Chop fresh basil leaves, if you have them, and stir them in just before serving. Serve with crackers. Makes about 2 cups.

BARBECUE CHICKEN

This is baked barbecue chicken that uses ketchup. In the oven, it won't burn. But a hot grill would burn any tomato-based substance. If you're eager to grill, marinate the chicken in the Best Mustard Vinaigrette on page 54.

Using whole chickens in this dish allows diners a choice, and bone-in chicken give makes a flavorful sauce. Even if you substitute chicken pieces (thighs and breasts is a good mixture), cook them bone-in. The cooked dish freezes well. Reheat, covered, at 350 degrees.

2 CHICKENS, CUT UP, OR THE EQUIVALENT PIECES TO SERVE 10 PEOPLE

1 TEASPOON SALT

1 TEASPOON (FRESHLY GROUND) BLACK PEPPER

1/4 CUP VEGETABLE OIL

3 LEMONS

2 TABLESPOONS VINEGAR

1 CUP KETCHUP

2 TABLESPOON SUGAR OR HONEY

2 TABLESPOONS WORCESTERSHIRE SAUCE

1/4 TEASPOON CRUSHED RED PEPPER FLAKES, OR TO TASTE

If you're cutting up the chicken yourself, or asking your meatcutter to do it, cut the leg and thigh apart and cut the whole breast into four pieces. Remove the skin, if desired.

Heat oven to 350 degrees. Place chicken on a large baking dish, or in two 9-by 13- baking dishes, and sprinkle it with salt and pepper. Drizzle with vegetable oil.

Squeeze juice from lemons into a medium bowl. Add remaining ingredients. Pour over chicken and cover tightly with lid or foil. Cook chicken 30 minutes. Remove cover from chicken and cook 20 to 30 minutes more, or until chicken is cooked through. Serves 10.

TRUE GRITS

The best grits to use for this (and any authentic grits or polenta dish) is Weisenberger grits. Weisenberger is one of the oldest mills in the country and it makes coarse-ground grits from Kentucky-grown corn. You can taste the grits in many of Louisville's best restaurants, and buy the grits for yourself in some finer supermarkets, at the web site www.weisenberger.com or by calling (800) 643-8678.

In the event you have leftovers, chill them, slice them and fry the slices gently in vegetable oil  to brown the edges and warm them through.

2 CUPS GRITS, PREFERABLY WEISENBERGER GRITS

1 TEASPOON SALT

3 CUPS MILK

1/2 CUP BUTTER

2 CLOVES GARLIC, PEELED AND MASHED WITH THE SIDE OF A KNIFE (OPTIONAL)

4 EGGS, BEATEN

2 CUPS GRATED SHARP CHEDDAR CHEESE

Butter a shallow 2- or 3-quart casserole.

Combine grits, 4 cups water and salt in a large pot set over high heat. Stir in milk. Bring the mixture to a boil, stirring very often, reduce heat to simmer and cook, stirring often, until very thick, about 15 or 20 minutes.

Combine butter and garlic in a small saucepan over low heat. Melt butter and keep on the heat until garlic becomes aromatic. Remove garlic cloves and stir butter into grits. Beat 1 cup of grits into eggs, then turn the eggs back into grits and stir to blend. Remove grits from heat and stir in 1 1/2 cups cheese until blended. Pour into casserole and sprinkle with remaining cheese. Bake at 400 degrees until brown around the edges. Or refrigerate (to make a firmer grits mixture) until thoroughly chilled, then bake at 350 degrees for 1 hour. Grits may be frozen before cooking; for best results, thaw in the refrigerator before baking. Serves 8.

FAVORITE GREEN BEAN SALAD

One of my favorite standby salads is this green bean salad with walnuts and feta cheese. It travels anywhere, can be made ahead, and tastes delicious. Feta cheese, toasted walnuts, and red onions make a salad so delicious that people return to the buffet table for it. The amount of dressing in this recipe coats the beans lightly, and some people have told me it's the perfect amount. If you like a lot of dressing, however, feel free to make and add more.

1 CUP CHOPPED WALNUTS
2 POUNDS GREEN BEANS
1 TABLESPOON SALT
1 RED BELL PEPPER
4 TO 8 OUNCES FETA CHEESE
1/2 TO 1 CUP DICED RED ONION
5 TABLESPOONS OLIVE OIL
1 1/2 TABLESPOONS BALSAMIC OR OTHER VINEGAR
1/2 TEASPOON (FRESHLY GROUND) BLACK PEPPER

Toast the walnuts in a 350-degree oven for 15 minutes, or until they are light brown and smell toasty. Set aside to cool.

Bring a large pot of water to boil over high heat (cover it to make it boil faster). Rinse and trim green beans as necessary. I cut them in halves or thirds to make them easier to serve from a buffet line. When water boils, add 2 teaspoons salt, then add the beans. Cook uncovered for 5 minutes, reducing the heat when the water returns to a boil.

Meanwhile dice onion and crumble feta cheese. Dice red pepper.

When the beans have cooked, rinse them in cold water until cold. They should be bright green and barely tender. Drain well and pat dry to make sure the dressing will adhere.

Combine olive oil, vinegar, remaining teaspoon of salt and pepper in a small bowl or jar. Stir or shake to dissolve salt. Toss the beans with dressing, add half of the cheese, walnuts, red peper and onions and toss again to distribute. Put the beans on a serving platter and scatter remaining cheese, pepper, walnuts and onions over the top.

Serves 8 to 10.

### CHOCOLATE CHIP PECAN PIE

Derby Pie is made by a company that has trademarked the name and has spent at least two generations making basically one thing: a chocolate nut pie. Needless to say, they have it down. They make a wonderful pie that has a perfect ratio of crust to filling and no bourbon. At the small pie factory two workers spend some of their week sitting at a small table sorting through the walnuts looking for bits of shell—they always find some. You can order their pies from www.derbypie.com.

Nevertheless, scores of chocolate chip pie recipes circulate around Louisville with various names, including Horse Race pie, Triple Crown pie—you get the picture. Some contain bourbon, some contain pecans. They're all pretty good. We especially like this one.

1/2 CUP BUTTER

2 EGGS

1 CUP SUGAR

2 TABLESPOONS BOURBON

3 TABLESPOONS CORNSTARCH

1 CUP FINELY CHOPPED PECANS

1 CUP (6 OUNCES) SEMI-SWEET CHOCOLATE MORSELS

1 (9-INCH) UNBAKED PIE SHELL

Melt butter and set aside. In a medium bowl, beat eggs just to break them up but not get them too frothy. Gradually add sugar, mixing just until blended. Stir in butter and bourbon. Blend in cornstarch. Stir in pecans and chocolate chips. Pour into pie shell. Bake in a 350-degree oven for 45 to 50 minutes. Cool 1 hour before serving. If the pie cools completely, warm it for 15 minutes at 350 degrees. Pie freezes well. It's best served with unsweetened real whipped cream. Serves 8.

# SATURDAY—DERBY DAY

Cooking starts early on the first Saturday in May.

As unlikely as it may seem, Churchill Downs is tucked into a rather urban neighborhood in southern Louisville, well within the city limits with all the limited access that implies. Everyone who lives nearby turns his or her yard into a parking lot, picking up a few extra dollars and inadvertently causing multiple block parties of their own. Hearty breakfasts are expected in the South End—and by many others who are working to support the Derby, from the paperboys in the parking lots to the media in town covering the event.

Those who attend the race will have a somewhat more leisurely pace. They'll eat brunch—something hearty because there's no desire to leave their seats for food when there are bets to be placed and handicapping to be done.

Just as brunchers are leaving for the track in late morning, others finalize plans for parties with friends and neighbors, fellow workers, family. Derby rivals the winter holidays as a time when Louisvillians plan big parties as pay-back or simply as their annual celebration. These parties take place in late afternoon and early evening, when the races are being run. Hosts usually have televisions in various rooms around the house. Hard-core race fans find their permanent seats. Others drift in and out of the room to check on what's happening. At these parties, practical party foods appear as often as traditional Derby foods.

In cities across the country, people who used to live in Louisville, or want to live in Louisville at least once a year, or who love horse racing more than life, are preparing their Kentucky dishes to impress their friends, and impress upon them how important these two minutes can

DERBY DAY BRUNCH
  Mimosas and bloody Marys
  Tomato aspic
  Shrimp salad
  Chicken salad with boiled dressing
  Benedictine salad
  Sally Lunn
  Secret strawberry shortcake
  Bourbon ball torte

DERBY DAY POT LUCK
  Mint juleps for a crowd
  Kentucky burgoo
  Shrimp dill spread
  Country ham balls
  Lemon marinated asparagus
  Chicken artichoke hot brown
  Chocolate bourbon charlotte

OUT OF TOWN DERBY PARTY
  Benedictine
  Country ham
  Biscuits
  Asparagus dippers
  Cheese torte
  Derby squares

## DERBY DAY BRUNCH

### MIMOSAS

Mimosas are a favorite brunch libation, associated with Derby only because brunches are such a prevalent way of entertaining. Be sure to offer non-alcoholic libations, too. Two tablespoons equals one ounce.

2 OUNCES CHAMPAGNE
1 1/2 OUNCES ORANGE JUICE
1/2 OUNCE GRAND MARNIER (ORANGE LIQUEUR)

Combine the ingredients in a champagne glass in the order listed. Serves 1.

### BLOODY MARYS

Bloody Marys show up at many brunches. Give this one a Louisville flair by ordering pickles from the Louisville Pickle company at www.kyagr.com, click on "buy Kentucky products" and then type "pickles" into the search window.

2 1/2 CUPS VODKA
5 CUPS SPICY TOMATO JUICE
2 TABLESPOONS FRESHLY SQUEEZED LEMON JUICE
2 TABLESPOONS WORCESTERSHIRE SAUCE
1 TEASPOON HOT SAUCE, SUCH AS TABASCO
1 1/4 TEASPOON CELERY SALT
1 1/4 TEASPOON SALT
CUT UP CELERY (TO STAND UP IN THE GLASS)
DILL PICKLE WEDGES (TO STAND UP IN THE GLASS)

Combine all ingredients except celery and dill pickle in a large pitcher. Chill (can be made days ahead). Fill glasses with ice, then fill with bloody Mary mix. Garnish with celery and pickle. Makes 10 6-ounce servings.

TOMATO ASPIC

In olden days, calves feet or pigs feet would be boiled to extract the gelatin and fresh tomatoes would be used for their juice in this most quintessential of Southern dishes: aspic. You can imagine how delightful cool aspic would taste in those days before air conditioning.

Modern convenience helps us get aspic to the table a little faster than the early days of the last century. Still, tomato aspic is considered quite refreshing and a welcome addition to a salad buffet.

Be advised, anything and everything can be added to aspic but be careful, its delicacy is something to admire.

The aspic can be prepared 48 hours in advance and kept refrigerated. Longer than that and the gelatin begins to toughen. Gelatin doesn't freeze well.

1/2 CUP FRESH LEMON JUICE

5 1/4-OUNCE PACKAGES UNFLAVORED GELATIN

46 OUNCES CANNED V8 JUICE

1 TABLESPOON RED WINE VINEGAR

1 TEASPOON TABASCO

3 TABLESPOONS SUGAR

SALT AND (FRESHLY GROUND) BLACK PEPPER TO TASTE

1 CUCUMBER, PEELED, SEEDED AND GRATED TO MAKE 1 CUP

Combine lemon juice and gelatin in small bowl and set aside to soften gelatin.

Heat V8 juice in a large saucepan until it simmers. Add gelatin mixture to hot V8 and stir until dissolved. Stir in vinegar, Tabasco, sugar, salt and pepper. Cool mixture, then refrigerate just until sides begin to set. Stir in 1 cup cucumber.

Use a non-stick cooking spray to grease a 8- to 10-cup ring mold or other mold and pour the aspic mixture into it. Refrigerate until set. Dip it in a sink of shallow warm water for 10 seconds. Using the pads of your fingers, gently pull the aspic away from the sides of the mold to loosen it. Turn the serving platter upside down on the aspic mold, then turn the platter and mold over together, so that the aspic plops onto the serving platter. Serves 12.

## SHRIMP SALAD

Such a small amount of grated onion may seem superfluous but I don't find it so. I like the little zing it brings but too much would just overwhelm the shrimp. Any cold salad like this is a welcome place for capers. Try it, you'll see.

1/2 CUP SOUR CREAM

1/2 CUP MAYONNAISE

2 TEASPOON GRATED ONION

2 TEASPOON DRY DILL

3 TABLESPOONS CAPERS (OPTIONAL)

1 TEASPOON CAYENNE PEPPER

1 TEASPOON SALT

3 POUNDS COOKED MEDIUM SHRIMP, PEELED AND DEVEINED

BIBB LETTUCE OR OTHER BUTTERHEAD LETTUCE

RED BELL PEPPER RINGS

Combine sour cream and mayonnaise in a bowl and stir to blend evenly. Add onion, dill, capers, cayenne and salt. Stir to blend. Add shrimp and stir to coat. Serve on a bed of salad greens with red bell pepper rings. Serves 8 to 10.

CHICKEN SALAD WITH BOILED DRESSING (For a crowd)

In traditional Southern homes, the boiled dressing had an honored place in the lexicon of salad presentations. No, it is not mayonnaise. Yes, you can use mayonnaise in this chicken salad (you may also add hard-cooked eggs). But the boiled dressing has a special flavor all its own—zippier than mayonnaise and eggier—and can make a wonderful difference on a salad that's been there, done that.

Dark meat makes the salad more flavorful; don't leave it out entirely.

DRESSING:

    6 EGGS
    1/4 CUP ALL-PURPOSE FLOUR
    3 TABLESPOONS SUGAR
    1 TABLESPOON SALT
    2 TEASPOONS DRY MUSTARD
    1 CUP APPLE CIDER VINEGAR (OR ANY VINEGAR)
    3 TABLESPOONS OLIVE OIL
    1/2 CUP HEAVY (WHIPPING) CREAM

SALAD:

    4 POUNDS BONELESS, SKINLESS CHICKEN (BREASTS AND THIGHS)
    SALT
    1 LARGE BUNCH CELERY

To make the boiled dressing: In a medium-size saucepan, beat the eggs to break them up. Beat in flour, sugar, salt and mustard. When the mixture is smooth, stir in 3/4 cup water, then vinegar. Put the mixture over low flame and add the olive oil. Stirring often, watch for the mixture to begin to thicken, then stir constantly. When it is very thick and lumpy, remove from the heat and beat aggressively until you whip out all the lumps. A whisk helps. Beat in the cream. Cool completely, then pour over chicken for salad.

To cook the chicken: You'll need wide, deep pots that can hold your chicken with water to cover. Put water in the pots and bring to a boil, adding salt to each. Add the chicken and when the water returns to the boil, reduce heat and simmer until chicken is cooked through—about 10 minutes for chicken breast halves, 20 or more for thighs. Drain, reserving water if you'd like it for cooking grits, making soup etc. and cool chicken.

Trim and wash celery. Dice it small—about 1/4-inch cubes or so if you have the patience. Scrape it into a large bowl as you do. Chop the cool chicken into approximately 1-inch cubes. Put them in the bowl with the celery. Mix with cold dressing. Taste for seasoning and add salt and pepper if necessary. Serves 15.

BENEDICTINE SALAD
   Named for the famed caterer, Jennie Benedict, not by her. This salad blends cucumbers with tangy sour cream in flavors reminiscent of Benedictine sandwich spread but more appropriate for the salad buffet.
   The rationale for seeding cucumbers: The seedy area holds lots of moisture which dilutes the flavors of the salad. Forego seeding the cucumbers if you wish—no biggy. But some hostesses think that seeding the cucumber makes a nicer salad presentation; the dressing doesn't get as watery.

   4 CUCUMBERS
   1 BUNCH GREEN ONIONS
   1 TEASPOON SALT
   1/2 TEASPOON CAYENNE PEPPER
   16 OUNCES SOUR CREAM

   Peel the cucumbers. Cut them in half lengthwise and use a teaspoon to scrape out the seeds. Cut the cucumbers in thin slices, transferring them to a bowl as you do so. Trim and mince green onions to make about 1/2 cup minced (less is fine). Put them in the cucumber bowl. Sprinkle with salt and cayenne. Add sour cream and stir to combine. Serves 15.

## SALLY LUNN

Sally Lunn purportedly gets its name from an English lass in Bath, who cooked a lovely yeast bread that was tender, a little rich, with almost a cake-like texture. It is said to have made its way to Virginia, and then all over the elegant South, wherever households could afford eggs, butter and sugar to go in it.

> 1 CUP MILK
> 1/2 CUP BUTTER
> 1/3 CUP SUGAR
> 2 TEASPOONS SALT
> 4 EGGS
> 1 PACKAGE ACTIVE DRY YEAST
> 4  CUPS SIFTED ALL-PURPOSE FLOUR

Combine milk, butter, sugar and salt in a small saucepan over medium heat and warm until the butter melts, stirring occasionally to dissolve sugar and salt. Allow it to cool to lukewarm. Beat the eggs until they are well blended. When the milk is lukewarm, add the yeast and stir to blend completely. Stir in eggs, then beat in flour (by hand or with a sturdy electric mixer). The batter should be shiny and too thick to be called a batter, but not quite thick enough to be called bread dough. Cover with plastic wrap and set aside in a warm place, or until it has risen to double in bulk. Beat it down again.

Grease a 9-inch tube pan or bundt pan. Turn dough into prepared pan, cover and let rise again until double in size.

Heat oven to 375 degrees. Bake the Sally Lunn 35 minutes or until nicely browned. Let rest in the pan 5 to 10 minutes, then turn out on a wire rack to cool. Serves 15.

## SECRET STRAWBERRY SHORTCAKE

Here's the secret: biscuit dough sometimes seems too cumbersome for tender, seasonal strawberries. Though biscuit dough, or something like it, traditionally is considered the "shortcake" of strawberry shortcake, the fruit really shines with something much "shorter"—rich pie dough. "Shortness" comes from the tenderness imposed by the fat mixed with the flour (that is, shorter gluten strands). Sprinkle coarse sugar over these pie dough discs if you have it.

SHORTCAKE:

>1 EGG
>
>1 1/4  CUPS ALL-PURPOSE FLOUR
>
>2 TABLESPOONS SUGAR
>
>1/2 TEASPOON SALT
>
>1/2 CUP COLD BUTTER

STRAWBERRIES:

>2 QUARTS STRAWBERRIES
>
>1/2 CUP SUGAR
>
>1 TABLESPOON COINTREAU OR GRAND MARNIER, OPTIONAL
>
>1 PINT HEAVY (WHIPPING) CREAM, WHIPPED TO SOFT PEAKS

Beat egg well. Add 1 1/2 teaspoons water and beat to combine. In a bowl, place flour, sugar, and salt. Cut butter into 8  pieces. Add to flour and using a pastry blender or two knives (or a food processor fitted with a steel blade), cut butter into flour to achieve the texture of a very fine meal. Drizzle in the eggs and stir briskly to moisten all the flour. The mixture should hold together when you press it with your fist, if not, add another teaspoon or two of water. Form the mixture into a disc, press it about 1 inch thick, then wrap in plastic and chill for 30 minutes.

Roll the dough on a lightly floured surface or between pieces of plastic wrap until it is about 1/8- to 1/4-inch thick. Use a glass or empty can or other implement to cut the dough in 3-inch rounds and transfer to a baking sheet. They can be placed very close together. Chill until the oven is preheated.

Heat the oven to 400 degrees. Sprinkle discs with sugar, coarse sugar if you have it. Place in the oven and cook 15 minutes, or until just beginning to brown. Remove and cool.

To make strawberries:

Remove and discard hulls. Cut fruit in smallish pieces and put them in a bowl. Sprinkle occasionally with sugar. Stir in Cointreau if using and allow the strawberries to chill 1 hour or more.

To serve:

Place a pastry disc on a plate. Top with a large spoonful of strawberries. Top with another disc. Add a dollop of freshly whipped cream. Serves 6.

**BOURBON BALL TORTE**

This variation on a flourless torte is flavored with bourbon to give a Kentucky flavor. Use brandy or rum if you prefer.

1 POUND SEMISWEET (OR BITTERSWEET) CHOCOLATE
1 CUP UNSALTED BUTTER
6 TABLESPOONS BOURBON (SUBSTITUTE COFFEE OR HEAVY CREAM, IF DESIRED)
9 EGGS, SEPARATED
1 1/4 CUPS SUGAR
1 TEASPOON SALT
1 TEASPOON CREAM OF TARTAR
1 PINT HEAVY (WHIPPING) CREAM

Generously butter a 10-inch springform pan (a pan where the hinge on the sides releases the bottom). Heat oven to 350 degrees.

If you're using block chocolate, break or cut it up into bits, no bigger than 1 ounce each. Combine it with butter and melt in a bowl set over a saucepan of warm water on low heat (or heat in the microwave on medium) Stir often until smooth. Stir in the bourbon. Stir until smooth and cool slightly.

Beat the egg yolks in a medium-size mixing bowl until very light. Gradually sprinkle in 1 cup sugar as you continue beating. Gently fold in the chocolate mixture.

In a large bowl, use clean beaters to beat egg whites until foamy. Add salt and cream of tarter and begin beating again, adding 1/4 cup sugar in a stream, beating until the egg whites form stiff peaks. Spoon a mound of egg whites into chocolate mixture and stir it in. Pour chocolate over egg whites and gently fold the chocolate into the whites until no white streaks remain. Pour into prepared pan and tap on the counter two or three times to bring large bubbles to the top. Bake 50 minutes, or until the center giggles a little but sides don't. The cake will rise, fall and the top will crack; that's normal, this being a modified souffle. Let cool on a rack 20 minutes. Run a knife blade around the edge of the pan to loosen the cake from the sides. Unhinge the cake pan. Cool completely, then wrap the pan tightly in foil and chill until firm. This cake is easiest to slice when you dip the knife blade in hot water and wipe clean. Serves 16. Serve with unsweetened whipped cream.

$$\boxed{\text{DERBY DAY POT LUCK}}$$

**MINT JULEPS FOR A CROWD**

A story circulates in these parts, sometimes attributed to Henry Watterson, a Louisville newspaper editor during the Civil War, that goes something like this: To make a great mint julep, pick the tiniest leaves from the earliest spring mint and place it in the bottom of a sterling silver julep cup. Add a spoon full of sugar, and carefully crush the two together until the leaves are reduced to a paste and the mixture is syrup. Pack the glass full of shaved ice. Then throw all of it out and fill with bourbon.

To be sure, there are plenty of bourbon lovers who take their bourbon neat. And plenty more who take it on ice. Both will complain that a mint julep is a sweet, syrupy, dilute concoction that doesn't warrant words in print, much less an honored place at Derby festivities.

I disagree. I am a bourbon lover and I like mine room temperature. But I maintain that a great mint julep can be a bourbon-lover's second favorite drink, and an appropriate way to celebrate, with or without solid silver cups.

A good mint julep requires the most judicious use of mint and sugar. The sugar is only necessary to extract the juices from the mint. These are my proportions for a bourbon-y mint julep, one with a touch of sweetness and mint, but mostly tastes of bourbon. If, on the other hand, you're aiming for a sweet, syrupy, dilute concoction, use less bourbon.

Anything that calls for a gallon of bourbon might give you pause, but this mint julep recipe prepares you for a large party.

  1 CUP SUGAR
  1 BUNCH FRESH MINT (ABOUT 1 CUP PACKED)
  1 GALLON GOOD QUALITY BOURBON

To make simple syrup, combine sugar and 1 cup water in a saucepan. Place over high heat and bring to a boil, stirring the mixture to dissolve the sugar. Boil 5 minutes. Remove from heat and add washed mint (still on the stem, just stir it all in). Set aside for 24 hours. Strain the mixture into a jar and discard the mint. Refrigerated, the syrup with last for months.

Chill julep cups or glasses in the freezer before making juleps. Fill them with shaved or crushed ice. Add 1 1/2 teaspoons of mint syrup and 2 ounces of bourbon. Garnish with sprigs of mint, if desired. Makes 32 juleps.

KENTUCKY BURGOO

Burgoo is Kentucky's game stew, made with a little of everything and enough to feed a huge gathering, like the kind of crowds that attend the summer barbecues of Catholic churches in Western Kentucky. There, the burgoos are cooked and stirred so long that the soup is nearly as homogenous as gravy, with bits of corn or lima bean appearing once in a while and the meat reduced to shreds. If you have frozen, dressed squirrel or rabbit, or shank of venison, throw it into this; otherwise, store-bought meats will do the trick.

> 2 POUNDS BEEF SHORT RIBS
> 2 POUNDS LAMB SHANKS
> 2 MEATY HAM HOCKS
> 31/2 - TO 4-POUND CHICKEN
> 1 (4-POUND) HEN, OR SUBSTITUTE RABBIT
> 5 OR 6 MEDIUM POTATOES, PEELED AND DICED
> 3 OR 4 MEDIUM ONIONS, PEELED AND DICED
> 1 POUND CARROTS, TRIMMED AND DICED
> 2 GREEN PEPPERS, STEMMED SEEDED AND DICED
> 2 CUPS WHOLE CORN, FRESH, FROZEN OR CANNED
> 2 CUPS DICED OKRA
> 2 CUPS LIMA BEANS
> 1 CUP DICED CELERY
> 1 QUART TOMATO PUREE
> 2 TABLESPOONS SALT, OR TO TASTE
> 1 TABLESPOON (FRESHLY GROUND) PEPPER
> 1 TEASPOON CRUSHED RED PEPPER FLAKES, OR TO TASTE
> CHOPPED PARSLEY

Put all the meat in a large, deep pot and add 2 gallons cold water. Turn the heat to high and bring the water to a boil. Reduce to low and simmer gently, skimming any foam off the top, until the meat is falling from the bones, about 2 hours. Strain the broth and chill meat and broth separately. When the meat is cool enough to handle, separate it from the bone (much of this may have already happened); remove and discard skin, cartilage, fat and other pieces you want out of your soup, When the broth is cold, skim fat from the top and discard.

Combine meat and broth and return to the boil over high heat. Add remaining ingredients (except parsley) as you prepare them, stirring often. When the mixture boils, reduce heat and simmer 4 to 6 hours, adding water when necessary and stirring often. In the end, the meat should be thin shreds and the vegetables should be insignificant—at the very least the potatoes should disintegrate—with fragments of a few still visible. The mixture is almost like a thick meat gravy. Add chopped parsley just before serving. Serves at least 30. Improves on standing a day or two (refrigerated). Freezes well.

SHRIMP DILL SPREAD

Just enough shrimp to make an elegant and popular dip without making it prohibitively expensive.

3  8-OUNCE PACKAGES CREAM CHEESE, SOFTENED
1  8-OUNCE CARTON SOUR CREAM
1/2 SMALL ONION, GRATED OR CHOPPED FINE
1 TABLESPOON DRY DILL
1/2 TEASPOON CAYENNE
1/2 TEASPOON SALT
1/2 TO 3/4 POUND SHRIMP, PEELED AND COOKED

Beat (or use a food processor) cream cheese until smooth. Add sour cream and beat to incorporate in cheese. Add onion, dill, cayenne and salt and beat to blend. Chop shrimp fairly small and stir into dip. Serve with crackers or French bread slices. Makes about 4 cups.

COUNTRY HAM BALLS

Everyone who buys a country ham needs to know what to do with leftover pieces and shards. This is a recipe that takes care of those pieces, and in the early days, people put the meat through a grinder. These days, most people just use the food processor. If you don't have stray ham bits, just buy ham at the deli or in the meat department. But if you buy a ham for Christmas or Easter, freeze the trimmings for this sweet-salty-sour Derby cocktail-party dish.

2 POUNDS COOKED COUNTRY HAM, GROUND
1 POUND UNCOOKED PORK SAUSAGE
2 CUPS DRY, UNSEASONED BREADCRUMBS
2 EGGS
1/2 TO 1 CUP MILK
2 CUPS BROWN SUGAR
1 CUP WHITE VINEGAR
1 TABLESPOON PREPARED DIJON MUSTARD

Combine ham, sausage, and breadcrumbs and use the side of a fork to cut them together. Beat the eggs slightly and stir them into the mixture briefly. Add 1/2 cup milk and mix with your hands. When the mixture is moist—add more milk if necessary—and can be formed into balls, shape into balls about the size of a walnut. (You can freeze the balls at this point).

Mix the brown sugar, vinegar and mustard in a small saucepan. Add 1 cup water and bring to a boil, stirring constantly, over medium-high heat. Heat oven to 350 degrees.

Spread the ham balls in a shallow baking pan and pour vinegar sauce over them. Bake for 45 minutes, basting occasionally. Makes about 8 dozen.

## LEMON-MARINATED ASPARAGUS

Asparagus in any form is welcome on a Derby table. This recipe is not only easy, it's delicious. The marinade can be used to dress nearly any vegetable or salad. Replace the asparagus with green beans if you like.

> 1 1/2 POUNDS ASPARAGUS
> 3 TABLESPOONS FRESH LEMON JUICE
> 3/4 TEASPOON SALT PLUS A LITTLE MORE FOR COOKING ASPARAGUS
> LOTS OF (FRESHLY GROUND) PEPPER
> 1/2 CUP GOOD QUALITY OLIVE OIL

Trim the dry ends of asparagus stalks and any woody stalk (1 or 2 inches). Peel any but the thinnest stalks.

Put about 2 inches of water in a wide (10- or 12-inch) skillet, salt the water and cover. Bring to a boil over high heat and add the asparagus, spreading it out so that if any asparagus is out of water, it is only part of the top layer. Boil the asparagus from 1 to 12 minutes, uncovered, or until the spears are bright green and easily pierced with the point of a sharp knife. Thin spears take less time, thick spears longer.

Remove from heat, drain immediately and rinse with cold water until the asparagus is cool. Spread the stalks on toweling and pat dry (they'll absorb water and seem soggy if you don't). Chill if not using immediately (wrap in a towel before placing in plastic bag).

Mix lemon juice, 3/4 teaspoon salt and pepper in a small jar with a tight fitting lid and shake to dissolve salt. Add olive oil and shake again vigorously to blend. Shake vigorously before spooning over blanched asparagus. Serves 6 for dinner; 8 to 12 as part of a buffet.

CHICKEN HOT BROWN

This easy-to-make casserole takes a few tips from the Hot Brown—tomatoes, poultry, cheese and bacon—and embellishes it with artichoke hearts. It can be assembled in advance and heated at the last minute. If you served it for dinner, it would probably serve 4 people, but it will serve at least 8 and probably more as part of large pot-luck buffet where everyone is contributing a dish.

3 SLICES BACON
1 PACKAGE FROZEN ARTICHOKE HEARTS (ABOUT 9 OUNCES), THAWED
4 BONELESS, SKINLESS CHICKEN BREAST HALVES
1 TEASPOON DRIED THYME
SALT AND PEPPER
1 POUND CANNED WHOLE TOMATOES, DRAINED
1/2 TO 1 CUP GRATED SHARP CHEDDAR CHEESE

Fry the bacon until crisp in a Dutch oven or deep stove-top casserole. Drain on absorbent paper. Pour out excess grease but don't wipe pot clean.

Heat oven to 400 degrees. Chop artichokes into small pieces and put them in the Dutch oven. Cut chicken into approximately 4 pieces each and place on top of artichokes. Sprinkle with thyme, salt and a generous amount of pepper.

Slice tomatoes and place the slices over the chicken. Combine grated cheese and crumbled bacon. Sprinkle over chicken and bake, uncovered, for 30 minutes, or until chicken is cooked and cheese is melted. Serves 4 as dinner, more on a buffet.

CHOCOLATE-BOURBON CHARLOTTE

For several decades, charlottes were the dessert of choice on Southern dessert tables because they could be made ahead and they were elegant, not to mention luscious. This chocolate charlotte has no peer. Some of the concepts may be new to you, but it is, in fact, simple to make and it freezes well, so you can make it weeks ahead.

If you don't like the flavor of bourbon, use rum. If you don't like the flavor of liquor, use cream.

1-POUND FROZEN OR BAKERY POUND CAKE
4 TABLESPOONS BUTTER
1 1/2 POUNDS SEMI-SWEET CHOCOLATE

    1/2 CUP BOURBON
    6 EGG WHITES
    1/2 TEASPOON CREAM OF TARTAR
    1/4 TEASPOON SALT
    2 CUPS SUGAR
    1 CUP HEAVY (WHIPPING) CREAM

ICING:

    1/2 POUND SEMI-SWEET CHOCOLATE
    1/4 CUP WHIPPING CREAM
    1 TABLESPOON BOURBON

Line a 2 1/2-quart souffle dish or bowl with plastic wrap. Slice the pound cake thinly and place slices vertically around the sides of the dish. They should slightly overlap. Place 2 layers of pound cake in the bottom, cutting it to fill any gaps. Set aside.

Melt butter and chocolate in a small saucepan set in a pan of hot water or in a microwave set on medium. Chocolate does not like high heat, so be gentle. Stir often so that it melts evenly. When the mixture is smooth, stir in the bourbon and set aside.

Beat egg whites until frothy with cream of tartar and salt. In a deep saucepan, combine sugar with 1 cup water and bring to a boil, stirring. Put the top on, turn the heat to low and simmer 3 minutes. Remove the top and bring to a boil again, cooking until large bubbles form and the mixture forms a soft ball when a small bit is dropped into cold water—about 240 degrees on a candy thermometer.

Begin beating the egg whites and pour the syrup in slowly in a constant stream. Don't beat too hard or the syrup will spray. After you've worked in the syrup, continue to beat the mixture until it has cooled to room temperature (you can put the bowl in cold water to speed the process).

Beat the cream until stiff peaks form. Fold the egg whites into the chocolate mixture gently but swiftly, then fold in whipped cream, folding until no white streaks remain. Scrape into pound cake-lined dish, cover with plastic and freeze.

To make icing: Combine chocolate and cream in a small saucepan set in a pan of hot water or in a microwave set on medium. Stir often so that it melts evenly. When the mixture is smooth, stir in the bourbon. Turn the charlotte on a serving plate and peel off the plastic wrap. Put thin strips of parchment or plastic wrap around the bottom of the charlotte to catch drips. Pour glaze over the top of the charlotte, spreading to cover the surface evenly. Remove drip strips. Chill or freeze until ready to serve. Serves 10 or more.

## OUT-OF-TOWN DERBY PARTY

**BENEDICTINE**

Ah! Benedictine! Most of the world thinks of it as a liqueur. In Louisville, we know it is a sandwich spread named after the eminent caterer of the early 20th century, Jenny Benedict, who is said to have served it. These days, any mix of cucumber and onion will work—some Louisville restaurants sell a chunky Benedictine as a sandwich filling, but it's traditionally served as a thin layer on crustless tea sandwiches.

8 OUNCES CREAM CHEESE

1 MEDIUM CUCUMBER

2 TO 3 TEASPOONS FINELY GRATED ONION

DASH OF CAYENNE

1/4 TEASPOON SALT, OR MORE TO TASTE

MAYONNAISE

Beat cheese with a mixer until smooth. Peel cucumber and put half of it in a blender. Blend until smooth. Beat it into the cheese until smooth. Add a little onion to taste, adding more if you like. The cheese should be spreadable. If it isn't, blend a little more cucumber and add it to the cheese. Add cayenne and salt to taste and add enough mayonnaise to make it the texture you like. Some people give the spread a faint green tint by adding a drop or two of green food coloring. Serve as a sandwich spread (for tea sandwiches), as a dip (may need more thinning) for vegetables or crackers. Makes about 1 1/4 cups.

**COUNTRY HAM**

Country ham is a fresh ham that has been buried in salt (which draws out the moisture that would otherwise allow it to spoil), then it is aged and often smoked briefly. To search for a ham that is not salty or strong is a little beside the point. How strong, and how salty, is a matter of much discussion in many Southern households, where the ham might be used as a seasoning, served on rolls or biscuits, or sliced and served for breakfast.

To be sure, this type of ham is an acquired taste and not for everybody. I happen to love it—no, crave it—and always use thinly sliced ham on my cocktail buffet tables. During a Kentucky History unit in my child's fourth grade Montessori class, most of the children ate the ham and many came back for more, so don't under-estimate your guests.

If you'd rather order a ham all cooked and sliced for you (a very practical and reliable choice), you'll find beautiful examples of the curing art at: www.meachamhams.com and www.fatherscountryhams.com.

To cook country ham:

Many ham owners foist off the responsibility of cooking ham. They'll take it to a butcher or a baker and pay to have the job done. Actually, preparing ham is a cinch. Slicing is another matter, and is easiest with a meat slicer. A large, sharp knife will work in a pinch.

Scrub the ham under running water using a stiff brush. Saw the hock off the ham so that it will fit into the pan (slice it off about 4 inches from the end of the hock, where the leg widens out and begins to get meaty). Place the ham in a deep pot (stock pot or canning pot) and cover with water. Soak the ham, changing the water daily, about 36 hours for hams up to 12 months old, 3 days for hams over a year. Hams less than 6 months old do not need soaking.

Drain ham, discarding soaking water. Place ham in the same pot and cover with water. Cover pot and bring water to a boil (this will take 30 minutes or more). Reduce heat to barest simmer and cook 4 hours (a large ham—16 or more pounds—will take 4 1/2 or 5; the internal temperature should be about 140 degrees). Turn off the heat and cool, covered, in the cooking liquid. Remove ham from liquid.(Ham broth can be refrigerated or frozen and used for cooking greens, rice, or soup.)

Remove skin and most of the fat from the ham by running your fingers under-neath, then trimming with a knife. Starting at the hip end, reach in and pull out the small bones. Once the small bones have been removed, find the large hip bone running through the ham. Use a knife to slit down the ham, running parallel to the large bone. Open the ham, grab the bone and twist to pull it out. Use a boning knife, if necessary, to slice through the tendon holding the bone.

Trim very dark or hard pieces of meat (use them to season broth, if desired). Wrap the ham tightly in plastic wrap. Put it in a large bowl, place a plate on top and weight it with bricks or cans. Refrigerate 8 hours, or several days. Slice ham as thinly as possible with a long, sharp knife, an electric knife, or, preferably, a meat slicer.

BISCUITS

Buttermilk gives incredible flavor to any quick bread, biscuits and pancakes especially. But many homes don't have buttermilk. Not to worry; biscuits made with "sweet milk" are delicious, too. Whole milk is best in this recipe, making more tender biscuits.

White Lily is a soft, Southern flour that makes tender biscuits.

1 3/4 CUP ALL-PURPOSE FLOUR, PREFERABLY WHITE LILY
1 TABLESPOON BAKING POWDER
1/2 TEASPOON SALT
6 TABLESPOONS BUTTER
3/4 CUP MILK
MELTED BUTTER

Heat oven to 450 degrees.

Combine flour, baking powder, and salt in a bowl. Cut butter in 6 chunks and add to bowl. Use a pastry blender or 2 knives to cut the butter into the flour until the mixture resembles coarse meal. Add milk and stir quickly until the dough comes free from the sides. Turn onto a lightly floured counter top and knead quickly, 6 or 8 times, until the dough smooths out enough to be rolled. Roll with a floured rolling pin to desired thickness (the smaller the biscuit cutter, generally the thinner the dough). Our 1 1/2-inch biscuits are rolled about 3/4-inch thick. Place almost but not quite touching in a baking pan and brush with melted butter, if desired. Bake 12 to 15 minutes, or until the top is lightly brown. Makes 10.

## ASPARAGUS DIPPERS

As many children know, fresh asparagus is a great finger food, and is very welcome at a springtime cocktail party. Asparagus is sort of like shrimp, though—as much as you provide, people will eat.

75 MEDIUM ASPARAGUS SPEARS (ABOUT 4 OR 5 BUNCHES)
1/2 CUP GOOD-QUALITY OLIVE OIL
2 TABLESPOONS WINE VINEGAR, OR VINEGAR OF CHOICE
1 CLOVE GARLIC, OR 1/2 TEASPOON, MINCED
1 TEASPOON SALT
1/2 TEASPOON (FRESHLY GROUND) PEPPER

Wash the asparagus and trim the ends so that the asparagus is about 6 inches long. Bring 1 inch water to boil in a wide skillet. Lay asparagus in skillet about 2 or 3 layers deep. Cook until bright green, turning the asparagus with tongs occasionally so that all are exposed to the water. Lift the asparagus from the water and drain on cloth towels (the asparagus should still be fairly firm). Repeat with remaining asparagus.

Combine olive oil, vinegar, minced garlic, salt and pepper and shake or stir to dissolve salt. Place the dip in a bowl and surround with asparagus. Serves 20 or more as a cocktail snack

## CHEESE TORTE

There's a version of this torte on every table in Louisville at least once during Derby. Many caterers use one type or another. It's pretty and it freezes well.

16-OUNCES EXTRA SHARP CHEDDAR CHEESE, GRATED AND AT ROOM TEMPERATURE
1 CUP PECANS, CHOPPED
1/2 MEDIUM ONION, MINCED FINE
2 TO 3 TABLESPOONS MAYONNAISE
2 8-OUNCE PACKAGES CREAM CHEESE, SOFTENED
1/3 CUP CHUTNEY
1/2 TEASPOON CAYENNE PEPPER
3 SLICES BACON
1/3 CUP FROZEN CHOPPED SPINACH
1 CLOVE GARLIC, MINCED, ABOUT 1/2 TEASPOON
1/2 TEASPOON SALT
1/4 TEASPOON OREGANO

Line a 1-quart dish with a flat bottom and straight sides with plastic wrap. In a bowl, combine softened cheddar cheese with pecans, onion and enough mayonnaise to hold mixture together. Spread half this mixture over bottom of dish. Chill the dish, but not the extra cheese.

In another bowl, combine 8 ounces cream cheese with chutney and cayenne. Blend thoroughly. Spread over cheddar cheese mixture. Chill.

Cook bacon until crisp, drain, then crumble. Meanwhile, thaw spinach and squeeze to remove all water. Combine in a bowl with remaining cream cheese, crumbled bacon, garlic, salt and oregano. Blend. Spread over chutney mixture. Top with remaining cheddar cheese mixture. Cover with plastic wrap overhang. Refrigerate or freeze until ready to use. If frozen, thaw overnight in refrigerator. Serves 20 to 30. Serve with crackers.

## DERBY SQUARES

An easy-to-make bar cookie that can feed lots of people, this recipe resembles the chocolate-nut pie associated with Derby time in Louisville.

PASTRY CRUST:

    2 CUPS FLOUR

    1 CUP LIGHT BROWN SUGAR

    1/2 CUP BUTTER, SOFTENED

TOPPING:

    1/2 CUP BUTTER

    1 CUP SUGAR

    2 EGGS

    1 TEASPOON VANILLA OR 2 TABLESPOONS BOURBON

    1/4 TEASPOON SALT

    1 CUP SEMI-SWEET CHOCOLATE MORSELS (6 OUNCES)

    1 CUP CHOPPED WALNUTS

Heat oven to 350 degrees. Mix flour, sugar and butter in a bowl, beating until evenly blended. Pat into a 9- by 13-inch baking pan and bake for 10 minutes.

For the filling, beat butter and sugar. Add eggs, vanilla and salt and beat to blend. Stir in chips and nuts and pour over crust. Bake 30 minutes, or until center is set. Cool and cut into squares. Makes 30 squares.

# SUNDAY—AFTER DERBY DAY

The morning after.

The day after Derby rivals New Year's Day in its languorous attitudes, its nostalgia and relief.

It's common for people in Louisville to work through Derby, entertaining company for business or actually working as part of the infrastructure. They want to relax with friends.

We still need to eat after Derby, to gather for closure, to wind down, debrief. A little brunch helps us, and the few who linger, waiting for late flights. One more bite of Kentucky goodness, and then, next year...

DAY-AFTER BRUNCH
> Turkey hash with country ham
> Simple salad
> Corn cakes or waffles
> Swedish cream with strawberries

---

### TURKEY (OR CHICKEN) HASH

Hash is the clever use of leftover meat. How turkey hash and corn cakes came to be associated with Kentucky, I don't know, but the link is indelible. There are many different interpretations of turkey hash—one resembles the interior of a chicken pot pie, only much meatier. Others are drier.

You can bake the turkey breast several days ahead or buy precooked authentic turkey or chicken at the supermarket. This entire dish can be cooked two days ahead of serving and refrigerated. Reheat in a 300-degree oven or in the microwave.

3 MEDIUM BAKING POTATOES

SALT

2 TABLESPOONS VEGETABLE OIL

1 ONION

1/2 POUND MINCED COUNTRY HAM

1 POUND (3 TO 4 CUPS) COOKED TURKEY MEAT OR CHICKEN MEAT

1/2 TEASPOON (FRESHLY GROUND) BLACK PEPPER

1/2 TEASPOON CAYENNE PEPPER, OR TO TASTE

3 CUPS TURKEY OR CHICKEN BROTH OR A COMBINATION

5 TABLESPOONS ALL-PURPOSE FLOUR

Peel potatoes, quarter them and place them in a medium saucepan with enough water to cover. Add 1 teaspoon salt, cover the pan and bring to a boil over high heat. Lower heat to simmer and cook until potatoes are barely tender, about 15 minutes. Drain and set aside.Meanwhile, heat vegetable oil in a wide, deep saucepan such as a Dutch oven. Chop onion and add to oil. Cook over medium-high heat, stirring occasionally, about 5 minutes. Cut potatoes into small cubes (less than 1/2 inch) and add to onion along with minced ham. Finely chop turkey and add to pan.

Season with salt, pepper and red pepper.

Combine broth and flour in a jar with a tight-fitting lid and shake vigorously to combine them evenly. Pour all at once into pan with turkey, increase heat to high and bring to a boil, stirring constantly.

When the mixture thickens, taste and correct seasoning. Scrape into a serving bowl (or chafing dish on low flame). Serve over corn cakes, waffles, biscuits, toast or toasted English muffins. Serves 8.

## CORN CAKES

Corn cakes are like cornbread pancakes and are better if made at the last minute. Silver-dollar-sized corn cakes can be frozen for a month. Reheat on a well-greased cookie sheet in a 350-degree oven. Larger pancakes don't taste as good reheated, but will do in a pinch. Brush them with butter for extra savoriness.

2 EGGS
1 1/2 CUPS BUTTERMILK OR MILK
1/4 CUP VEGETABLE OIL, PLUS A LITTLE MORE FOR GREASING THE PAN
1 CUP CORNMEAL
1 CUP ALL-PURPOSE FLOUR
1 TEASPOON SALT
2 TEASPOONS BAKING POWDER
DASH TABASCO OR OTHER HOT SAUCE (OPTIONAL)

Beat eggs in a large bowl. Add milk and oil and beat well. Add dry ingredients and beat. Add Tabasco, if desired. Thin with more milk, if necessary, until the mixture is the consistency of pancake batter.

Heat a little oil in a large skillet over medium-high heat. Add 1/4 cup batter and fry until bubbles appear all over. Turn and brown on the other side. Keep cooked corn cakes warm in a 300-degree oven, if desired.

Makes 12 cakes. To make smaller corn cakes, use a tablespoon to dip the batter out.

## SIMPLE SALAD

SALAD:

    4 HEADS BIBB LETTUCE

    2 OR 3 SLICES RED ONION

    2/3 CUP PECANS, TOASTED

LEMON DRESSING:

    1 LEMON

    1 CLOVE GARLIC, 1/2 TEASPOON MINCED

    1/2 CUP OLIVE OIL

    1 TEASPOON SALT

Separate leaves of Bibb, rinse and wrap in toweling to dry the leaves (you may put the towel-enclosed leaves in a plastic bag and hold them for a day or two).

Heat oven to 400 degrees. Toast nuts for 10 minutes, or until they smell fragrant.

Remove the rind of the lemon with a fine grater—be careful to get only the yellow part. Combine lemon rind with minced garlic and salt in a jar or bowl. Add olive oil and the juice from the lemon and shake or stir to dissolve salt. Taste the dressing and if it is too tart, add a little more olive oil and 1/2 teaspoon sugar.

Toss dry lettuce leaves with a little of the dressing and arrange the leaves on 8 plates. Sprinkle with pecans. Separate onion slices to make rings, and place a few rings on each salad. Dress with more dressing to taste. Serves 8.

### SWEDISH CREAM WITH STRAWBERRIES

Swedish cream is another popular and reliable (and delectable) Louisville dessert that goes well with any seasonal fruit, is not too sweet, and it's the easiest thing you've ever made. It goes well with fruits in season. Make it at Derby with strawberries, in July with blackberries and blueberries, and in August with peaches.

SWEDISH CREAM:

> 1 PACKAGE UNFLAVORED GELATIN (1 SCANT TABLESPOON)
>
> 3/4 CUP SUGAR
>
> 2 CUPS HEAVY CREAM
>
> 1/2 CUP MILK
>
> 2  8-OUNCE CARTONS SOUR CREAM
>
> 1 TEASPOON VANILLA

SAUCE:

> 1 QUART STRAWBERRIES
>
> 1 CUP SUGAR

Swedish cream: Sprinkle gelatin over 1/4 cup cold water and set aside to soften for about 5 minutes.

In a saucepan, combine the sugar, heavy cream, milk and gelatin. Heat and stir until sugar and gelatin are completely dissolved. Cool completely. Gradually add to sour cream, stirring constantly to combine completely. Add vanilla and stir to combine.

Spray a 2-quart mold or bowl with cooking spray. Pour cream into mold and chill. When ready to serve, dip the mold into warm water for 10 seconds, cover the top with a plate, then turn the whole thing over. Give a gentle shake if you have to until the mold plops onto the plate. Serve slices of cream on pools of strawberry sauce.

Strawberry sauce: Cut strawberries into small pieces and place in a non-reactive (stainless steel, enameled, glass) Add sugar and allow to stand about 20 minutes, to draw out some of the juice. Cook over medium-high heat, stirring constantly, until the mixture begins to boil.Reduce heat to simmer and cook about 10 minutes. Set aside until cool, then cover and refrigerate before serving.